BRUCE A. KUGLER

WARFARE

IN THE

SPIRITUAL

REALMS

Recognizing and Resisting
the Work of the Enemy in Your Life

WARFARE IN THE SPIRITUAL REALMS

Publisher's Cataloging-in-Publication data

Names: Kugler, Bruce A., author.

Title: Warfare in the spiritual realms: how to recognize and
resist the work of the enemy in your life / Bruce A. Kugler.

Description: Includes bibliographical references and index. |
Sherman, IL: Bruce A. Kugler, 2023.

Identifiers: LCCN: 2023912746 | ISBN: 979-8-9876214-0-0 (paperback) |
979-8-9876214-1-7 (ebook)

Subjects: LCSH Spiritual warfare. | Demonology. | Devil—Christianity. | Good and evil—Religious aspects—Christianity. | Christian life. | BISAC RELIGION / Christian Theology/ Angelology & Demonology | RELIGION / Christian Ministry / Counseling & Recovery | RELIGION / Christian Living / Spiritual Warfare
Classification: LCC BT975 .K84 2023 | DDC 235/.4—dc23

Table of Contents

INTRODUCTION

There is a war going on in the spiritual realms between two very powerful kingdoms, the Kingdom of God and the Kingdom of Satan. A battle is constantly raging between holy angels and demon spirits, seeking to control and influence people's lives and their eternal destinies. The Apostle Paul recognized that believers are involved in this spiritual war when he stated, "For our struggle is not against flesh and blood, but against the rulers, against the powers, against the world forces of this darkness, against the spiritual forces of wickedness in the heavenly places" (Eph. 6:12).

Unfortunately, there are unbalanced viewpoints when it comes to spiritual warfare. One viewpoint is that every problem is a result of demon spirits. Some attribute every spiritual problem, difficulty, or trial to Satan. Yet, it is false to believe that every psychological challenge, health issue, or temptation is caused by a demon spirit. Some also blame Satan and the demons for every sin they commit. Another unbalanced viewpoint is that demon spirits are not real and have no influence over people. Some contend that

belief in demon spirits was merely a way for ignorant people thousands of years ago to explain pain, suffering, and
why evil exists. Yet, this premise may lead to the errone-
ous conclusion that the problems attributed to demons in
the Bible were caused by psychological or medical issues.
The fact that there may have been an oversimplification
to the question of evil in the past is not a valid reason to
reject the reality of the spiritual realms and demon spirits,
because both were recognized by Jesus Christ in the Bible.

It is important to have a sound biblical understanding
of spiritual warfare. Yet, spiritual warfare has been virtu-
ally ignored by mainstream evangelical Christianity. Many
think it is an area reserved for missionaries, or perhaps
those ministering to individuals in witchcraft or Satanism. Most Christians have probably concluded that understanding spiritual warfare is not important in their own life.
Those who experience deep spiritual difficulties or problems are often counselled that the root cause of their problems is either an inability to conquer the flesh or a lack of
commitment to Christ. This could be true; however, many
never give serious consideration that their problems may
also be related to the activity of demon spirits.

Spiritual warfare is not merely the study of demon spirits. Of course, examining Satan's origin and organization is
important. Understanding the scope of Satan's activity and
how demons affect the believer are also crucial. The believer
cannot effectively engage in spiritual warfare without
examining such critical areas as the Armor of God, holy
angels, the blood of Jesus Christ, being filled with the Holy
Spirit, and the power of prayer. Victory in spiritual warfare
also requires an understanding of the difference between
the world, the flesh, and the Devil.

Some believe that to engage in spiritual warfare requires

a vast amount of knowledge and that only mature Christians should dare engage the enemy. Both beliefs are false. Those most likely to benefit from engaging in spiritual warfare are believers who are struggling in their spiritual life or are in bondage to sins which they have never been able to overcome. Understanding how these bondages develop and how they can be broken will be welcome information. Others will gain a rich understanding of how to effectively pray for friends and loved ones to receive Jesus Christ as Lord and Savior. Those who read and apply the materials in this book will have the knowledge and confidence to assist others in direct confrontation with the powers of darkness. Believers will find that engaging in spiritual warfare will add a new dimension in their relationship with God.

1

BREAKING SIN BONDAGES

I would like to tell you a true story. John's mother was a Christian who often prayed for him. However, by the time John was sixteen he was an atheist. He took pleasure in convincing others to turn away from Christianity. When John was nineteen, he began working in the slave trade in England. The year was 1744. John eventually became a captain on a slave ship. He participated in the brutality against the Africans. Death and cruelty on a slave ship were common. Approximately one-third of the slaves on the ships were women. Something that you are not often told in your school history books is that the officers and captains would often enter the hull of the ships to select women and then violate them. This was done on a regular and systematic basis. It shocks the modern conscience. Unfortunately, John participated in these activities. Even the hardened sailors on the ships were astonished at the depths of John's wickedness.

One night John's ship encountered a violent storm and began to sink. John could hear the screams of a sailor as he lost his life. During the night John cried out to God for mercy and the ship survived. The next day after the storm had passed, John had time to think about his experience.

After eleven hours of reflecting, he decided to receive Jesus Christ as his Lord and Savior. I want to emphasize that John made a very deliberate, considered, and informed decision. His decision was not the quick, emotional, or "Easy Believism" that is prevalent in so many churches in the United States today. That is, merely repeating a quick salvation prayer, without considering the cost, without repenting of sin, and without submitting to God. John was astonished at God's mercy. He even went back to his father and asked for forgiveness for his evil lifestyle.

Sometime later John needed money. He could not find a job so reluctantly he accepted a position on a slave ship. After several weeks, John stopped reading his Bible. He became careless in prayer and had no Christian fellowship. Eventually John found himself participating in the same kinds of evil as before. I am not going to go into detail on the extent of his sins against the Africans, especially the women. Suffice to say, John was a wretched human being before he was saved and by all human standards, he was a wretched human being after he was saved. John himself states, "I was now fast bound in chains; I had little desire and no power to free myself."[1] Do you ever feel like that yourself as a Christian? Having little desire and no power to free yourself from doubt, over-eating, negative thoughts, bitterness, drugs, violent thoughts, fear, coveting, lust, unforgiveness, complaining, worry, and other sins and strongholds. If you do, Satan has you right where he wants you. Most likely frustrated, discouraged, often miserable, and unusable by God. Yet it does not have to be that way. I am going to finish the story about John, but not right now.

Like many Christians today, John did not understand the difference between being forgiven of the "Penalty of Sin" and breaking the "Power of Sin" in his life. You must understand the difference between these two concepts. Let's first discuss being forgiven of the penalty of sin.

FORGIVENESS FROM THE PENALTY OF SIN

When a person receives Jesus Christ as his Lord and Savior, God forgives him of the penalty of sin. He receives a pardon and the Holy Spirit enters him. We must start here because if you do not have the Holy Spirit, you will have no power in your life. The engine of a car will not start unless there is a battery under the hood. Nothing else I explain in the coming chapters will matter if you do not get this part right.

There are three requirements to be forgiven of the penalty of sin and receive this pardon. First, you must admit that you have sinned. "For all have sinned and fall short of the glory of God" (Rom. 3:23). Some people have sinned a lot and others have sinned a little, but the fact remains that everyone has sinned against God at some point in their life. This includes me, you, and every person living on the earth.

Second, you must believe. You must believe the penalty of your sin is eternal punishment. "For the wages of sin is death" (Rom. 6:23). This not only means that a person's physical body will die because of sin, but that he also will be eternally separated from God in a place known as the Lake of Fire. You must also believe that Jesus Christ is the Son of God, that He died on a cross, shed His blood to pay the penalty for your sin, and arose from the dead. God took all your sins and placed them on Jesus Christ while He was on the cross. God then poured out all His wrath and all His judgment that should have been directed toward you and He directed that wrath and judgment on

His Son in your place. In other words, Jesus Christ took your punishment. Jesus Christ volunteered to be your personal substitute.

For my Muslim readers, please do not confuse what I mean when I say that Jesus Christ is the Son of God. There is only one God, not three. I am not saying that God had relations with Mary which produced Jesus Christ. Instead, what I am saying is that Jesus Christ is eternal; God exists in three persons who share the same essence or being. Jesus Christ is the personification of God in human flesh. Yet, there is only one God. I admit that this seems illogical and hard to explain. I believe this fact not because I fully understand it but because it is revealed in the Word of God. "For God so loved the world, that He gave His only begotten Son, that whoever believes in Him should not perish but have eternal life" (John 3:16).

The third requirement is that you must commit your life to Jesus Christ. You must confess Jesus Christ as Lord. "That if you confess with your mouth Jesus as Lord and believe in your heart that God has raised Him from the dead you will be saved" (Rom. 10:9). You must be willing to make Jesus Christ the Lord of your life. This means that Jesus Christ must be the boss of your life. Some would argue that you do not need to acknowledge and submit to Jesus Christ as Lord at the time of salvation. I would agree that you can be saved without knowing the full implications of the Lordship of Jesus Christ in your life. However, you cannot be saved if there is an area in your life that you refuse to surrender to Christ as Lord (boss).

Money is a good example. Money is often a stumbling block to being saved because it can be a form of greed and idolatry. You cannot serve God and money. So, if a person is not willing to let Jesus Christ be the boss on how they use their money (if money is their current god), the Holy Spirit may zero in on this issue when drawing the person for salvation. I have presented the Gospel in India. Hinduism has thousands of gods. When considering salvation, some are tempted to merely add Jesus as one of their gods. Thus, it needs to be made clear that Jesus Christ must be your one and only God.

Jesus Christ was making the same point when He dealt with the rich young ruler. You may recall, he asked Jesus Christ what he needed to do to obtain eternal life. Jesus told him that he needed to keep the commandments. The rich young ruler then asked Jesus, "Which ones?" Jesus then listed several commandments:

> "You shall not commit murder;
> You shall not commit adultery;
> You shall not steal;
> You shall not bear false witness;
> Honor your father and mother; and
> You shall love your neighbor as yourself."
>   (Matt. 19:18-20).

Notice the response of the rich young ruler:

> "The young man said to Him, 'All these things I have kept; what am I still lacking?' Jesus said to him, '*If you wish to be complete, go and sell your possessions and give to the poor, and you will have treasure in heaven; and come, follow Me.*' But when the young man heard this statement, he went away grieving; for he was one who owned much property. And Jesus said to His disciples, 'Truly I say to you, it is hard for a rich man to enter the kingdom of heaven'" (Matt. 19:21-23, emphasis added).

The rich young ruler was an intensely religious person. He claimed that he had kept all these commandments. Very impressive! Yet, Jesus zeroed in on the one area that he was not willing to surrender. He told the rich young ruler to sell his possessions and give the money to the poor and come follow Him. Unfortunately, he was not willing to obey Jesus Christ. When Jesus Christ is drawing a person for salvation, there is often a battle for control and submission in various areas of a person's life. For the rich young ruler, it was money. For others it may be a sexual habit, a job, a relationship, unforgiveness, or some other sin.

Committing your life to Jesus Christ also means that you must repent of your sin. "Unless you repent you will all likewise perish" (Luke 13:5). Repentance is telling God that you are sorry for your sin and that you are willing, by His help, to turn from sin. Let me tell you a story about a man named Dan. I have been involved in martial arts for many years. Dan was one of my sparring partners. One day while Dan and I were working out, he asked me what he needed to do to go to Heaven. I then explained the requirements for salvation. Dan admitted that he was a sinner. He believed the penalty of his sin was eternal punishment. He also believed that Jesus Christ died on a cross, shed His blood, paid the penalty for his sin, and arose from the dead. I then explained that he also needed to repent of his sin. A sad expression came to his face. Dan told me that he was not willing to repent. Since Dan was a friend and could be honest with me, I asked him, "Why not?" He told me that he was having sex with his girlfriend and did not want to stop. I believe Dan was willing to repeat a prayer, "Jesus come into my heart." However, repeating such a prayer when a person is not willing to repent of sin only gives a false sense of security in their salvation. The stumbling block for Dan was that he was not willing to repent of his sin.

Please do not misunderstand me. There is no requirement that a person must overcome certain sins to be saved. In fact, prior to salvation a person may have no power to overcome certain sinful habits and addictions. However, a person must repent of sin and be willing to allow Jesus Christ to help him to overcome. A person is responsible to submit and surrender to Jesus Christ. After salvation it is God's responsibility to provide the power of the Holy Spirit to overcome and conquer sin. For example, let's say you are sharing the Gospel with a person who has been an alcoholic for thirty years. The person was in the bars last week getting drunk. He candidly admits that he will most likely be in the bars next week also getting drunk. Can that person be saved? The person by his own admission cannot overcome his drunkenness. Fortunately, he does not need to overcome this sin prior to salvation. However, he does need to repent of his sin and be willing to let Jesus Christ help him overcome. The person must be willing to let Christ change him in areas where he cannot change himself. If the person is willing to take these steps, he can immediately be saved. On the other hand, if the person refuses to repent and is not willing to let Jesus Christ help him overcome sin, but intends to continue to get drunk in rebellion to the commandment of God, he cannot be saved at that time. Despite this, there is still hope. Through prayer by other believers the person may eventually come to the point in his life where he is willing to repent of his sin, submit to Jesus Christ, and receive the gift of salvation.

If you are sharing the Gospel, be sensitive to the Holy Spirit as to whether the person really understands the requirements for salvation. Do not be so quick to have the person merely recite a salvation prayer. You do not want to give the person a false sense of security.

PRAYER TO RECEIVE GOD'S OFFER OF A PARDON

I would like to invite you right now to accept God's offer of a pardon. If you would like to accept God's offer of a pardon, please pray this prayer. Remember, God examines the intention of your heart. It is not the precise words you use but your willingness to admit, believe, and commit your life to Jesus Christ. An example prayer to accept God's offer of a pardon is as follows:

> "God, I admit that I have sinned. I believe the penalty of my sin is eternal punishment. I believe that Your Son Jesus Christ died on a cross, shed His blood to pay the penalty for my sin, and arose from the dead. I commit my life to Jesus Christ. I submit to Jesus Christ as the boss and authority of my life. I repent of my sin. I confess Jesus Christ as my Lord. I accept Your offer of a pardon. Thank you. Amen."

For those of you who have just accepted God's offer of a pardon, the next important step is for you to be baptized. Jesus commanded that all who accept Him as Savior shall be baptized. "He who has believed and has been baptized shall be saved; but he who has disbelieved shall be condemned" (Mark 16:16). You have just prayed that Jesus Christ is going to be the Lord and boss of your life. Being baptized is one of the first tests of your obedience. It reveals whether you really meant what you just prayed. Find a Bible-believing church, talk to the pastor about your decision to accept God's offer of a pardon and request to be baptized.

FORGIVENESS OF ALL PAST, PRESENT, AND FUTURE SINS

If just now or previously you fulfilled all three requirements (admit, believe, and commit), something amazing happened. God forgave you of all your sins, past, present, and future. So, let's assume you accept God's offer of a pardon, and you are twenty-five years old. At that moment in time, God looks into your future and sees all of the sins that you will ever commit until the end of your life, and He forgives you of all of them. God then declares that you are perfectly righteous even though in practice you are not. God knows that you are not perfectly righteous. You know that you are not perfectly righteous. Your spouse and children definitely know that you are not perfectly righteous. Yet, God declares that you are perfectly righteous.

When my youngest daughter Claire was four years old if she did something extra good or nice, I would tell her, "You can now be six." She would then go around telling everyone, "My dad made me six." My wife finally asked me to stop it. She knew I was kidding, but she did not want my daughter confused. Of course, I have no power to make a four-year old six by just my word; however, God does have the power to declare a sinful person perfectly righteous. The Bible calls this the gift of righteousness and is referred to in the Book of Romans. "For if by the transgression of the one, death reigned through the one, much more those who receive the abundance of grace and the gift of righteousness will reign in life through the One, Jesus Christ" (Rom. 5:17). This is also why the Bible states that God no longer condemns the believer. "There is now no condemnation for those who are in Christ Jesus" (Rom. 8:1). If you have accepted God's offer of a pardon, God no longer condemns you. When you sin after salvation, the Holy Spirit will convict you, but He never condemns you. When the Holy Spirit convicts you, it is as if He puts His arms around you and says to you, "You can do better. I am here to help you. We can conquer this sin together."

INCREASED SPIRITUAL WARFARE AFTER SALVATION

At the time of your salvation, when you accept God's offer of a pardon, you will begin to experience increased spiritual warfare! The battle is not only against worldly influences and the flesh (some call it the sin nature), but also against Satan and an army of demon spirits. The Bible describes this adversary: "For our struggle is not against flesh and blood, but against the rulers, against the powers, against the world forces of this darkness, against the spiritual forces of wickedness in the heavenly places" (Eph. 6:12).

Satan has a strategy to destroy you. In Revelation 9:11, a demon spirit or perhaps Satan himself is referred to as "Abaddon" in Hebrew and "Apollyon" in Greek which is translated "Destroyer."[2] Satan wants to destroy you mentally, physically, financially, emotionally, and sexually. We know that in any physical war people get injured, scarred, and sometimes die. There are casualties in any physical war. Likewise in this spiritual warfare, some Christians will become casualties. As a result of unrepented sin and other strategies of the enemy, some Christians will experience unnecessary pain, demonic bondage, oppression, emotional instability, and premature death. Some Christians may attempt or even commit suicide. There is no limit on the extent the powers of darkness will try to push a person once certain doors are open. Furthermore, innocent people often get hurt. Children are often hurt by the sins of their parents and others. Some Christians will become casualties in this spiritual warfare because they never dealt with the power of sin in their lives and have opened the doors to the powers of darkness.

PURPOSE OF REPENTANCE AFTER SALVATION

After salvation why do you repent of sin? You have already been forgiven of the penalty of sin. You have been forgiven of all your sins, past, present, and future. When you are saved, your relationship with God has been established, but your fellowship is broken when you sin. For example, my daughter once lied to me. I was very disappointed. Yet she did not cease to be my daughter because she lied, but our fellowship was broken. She later apologized and our fellowship was restored. If you are truly saved (if you have accepted God's offer of a pardon) your relationship with God has been established, but your fellowship is broken when you sin.

The first reason you repent is to maintain your fellowship with God. The second reason you repent is to prevent the powers of darkness from creating a sin bondage in your life. In order for a demonic power to create a sin bondage, they need you to open a door for them. Flies do not get into a house unless a door is left open. When a believer sins and refuses to repent, he or she gives the powers of darkness permission to begin creating a sin or demonic bondage because of the opened door.

Let me give you an example. Let's assume someone hurt

you at church. The person said a rude and nasty comment and you are tempted with bitterness. At that moment you have a choice to either reject the temptation or give into the sin. Reject the lie that you are powerless to overcome. "No temptation has overtaken you but such as is common to man; and God is faithful, who will not allow you to be tempted beyond what you are able, but with the temptation will provide the way of escape also, so that you will be able to endure it" (1 Cor. 10:13). If you are truly saved and have the Holy Spirit residing in you, then you have the power to resist the temptation. You have the battery in the car. Thus, you should immediately reject the thought of being bitter at the person who hurt you.

Assume that you do not immediately reject this evil thought. Instead, you choose to dwell on the thought of bitterness and how much you despise the person. This poor choice results in cracking open a door to the powers of darkness. As soon as you sin, the Holy Spirit will convict you. You then have another choice. You can either repent of the sin or ignore the Holy Spirit. If you ignore the Holy Spirit this time, He will continue to be grieved. "Do not grieve the Holy Spirit of God by whom you were sealed for the day of redemption" (Eph. 4:30). If you continue to ignore the Holy Spirit, He will become quenched. "Do not quench the Spirit" (1 Thess. 5:19). At this point you are headed for trouble. What started out as a mere temptation or an isolated sin could become a sin bondage, a demonic bondage, and the bitterness will be very difficult to break. This is where many Christians are at in their spiritual life. It is similar to driving a car with the parking brake on. The car should be going seventy mph, but the parking brake is on, and you are only going five mph and wondering why.

Let me ask you a question. Do you feel there is a spiritual parking brake on in your life?

Once a demonic power is able to establish a sin bondage in your life, it grows like cancer and may affect other areas in your life. What started out as a bitterness problem may spread to other areas, including but not limited to, anger, jealousy, lust, over-eating, or lack of self-control. Your spiritual life never remains neutral. You are either growing closer to God or moving away. You are either shutting the doors to the powers of darkness or opening new doors.

CONSEQUENCES OF FAILING TO REPENT OF SIN

There will be significant consequences in your life for ignoring the Holy Spirit and failing to repent of sin. Initially you may notice that you have no love, joy, peace, or patience. You will be cut off from the fruit of the Holy Spirit. This is because the Holy Spirit is cutting you off to get your attention! He is trying to get you to notice the red flags. Your thought life may become immoral. Your mind will be like a garbage can. There will be strife, jealousy, frustration, and discontentment in your life. You will probably be miserable. If you continue down this path you will enter a phase of self-deception.

In the martial arts there are some people who try to develop the "Iron Hand." Every day they will thrust their hand into a bucket of sand. Over time, they increase the coarseness of the sand. Eventually they put little pebbles into the bucket and continue thrusting their hand into the bucket. The goal is to have their hand become callous and insensitive to pain so when they punch someone, they will not feel any pain.

Allowing the power of sin to control your life over time will result in you becoming insensitive and callous to the Holy Spirit. Some Christians will get to the point where they actually believe the sin they are committing is not really wrong. They will no longer feel convicted. This is how some Christians can look you straight in the eye and tell you:

> They are having sex with someone, whom they are not married to, and do not feel it is wrong.

> They have a steady diet of watching R-rated movies and playing violent video games and do not feel it is wrong.

> They gossip about or criticize their pastor and do not feel it is wrong.

> They give little or nothing to financially support the work of their church or missions when they could afford it and do not feel it is wrong.

> They do not have a burden for others to be saved and do not even pray for lost people and do not feel it is wrong.

In all of these examples, the person may honestly not believe or feel their actions are wrong. There could only be two reasons. First the Holy Spirit is not in them. They are not truly saved. The second reason could be that they have opened the doors to the powers of darkness and have become callous and insensitive to the Holy Spirit. You should not determine what is right or wrong on the basis of whether you feel convicted. You cannot trust your feelings because your conscience may be broken.

STEPS TO BREAK THE POWER OF SIN

You might be asking, "I know I am saved. I know that I have previously accepted God's offer of a pardon. I know the Holy Spirit is in me, but I have sin bondages in my life. How do I break them?" You begin to break the power of sin by submitting to God. "Submit therefore to God. Resist the devil and he will flee from you" (Jam. 4:7). You can resist Satan all you want, but if you have not submitted to God the devil will not flee. Your self-help, human will-power, or New Year's resolution is no match for the powers of darkness. Instead, there must be complete submission to God. There also needs to be repentance. "If we confess our sins, He is faithful and righteous to forgive us our sins and to cleanse us from all unrighteousness" (1 John 1:9).

What happens to many people is they get saved; they are forgiven of the penalty of sin; however, they go about their lives for months, even years, not daily repenting and renouncing their sin as the Holy Spirit convicts them. They are not dealing with the power of sin. So, sin begins to get a grip on their life. They eventually become miserable and cry out to God! Perhaps, they decide to rededicate their life to Christ. Don't deceive yourself! After years of allowing the power of sin to rule your life, you cannot merely rededicate your life and say a five second prayer, "Lord Jesus, I repent of all my sins for the last five years" and expect the power of sin to be instantly broken. That is a good start, but probably will not break the power of sin!

Breaking the power of sin requires allowing the Holy Spirit to place His searchlight on your heart and bring to your mind sins that you have committed in the past, but have failed to repent of. Then you must specifically repent of these sins. This is not a self-imposed guilt trip; instead, it is allowing the Holy Spirit to thoroughly deal with you. But it takes time. It might take days or weeks. But there is no other solution to break the power of sin and demonic bondages when the bondage was created by unrepented sin. Not dealing with the power of sin "today" will cause needless pain in your life "tomorrow," and needless pain in other people's lives around you.

I want to explain a tool that is in the Appendix. It is called the "Sinventory." It is a tool that can help you remember sins you have committed in the past but have long forgotten. These sins may be contributing to a spiritual bondage in your life. The Sinventory lists dozens of sins. For each sin, a Bible verse is quoted, and questions are provided for you to ponder to determine if you have committed this particular sin. The Sinventory can be used by the Holy Spirit to bring to your mind sins you have committed in the past but have never repented of.

Do not give into the temptation of repenting from most of your sins but keeping a few favorite ones. Unrepented sin is an open door in your life to the powers of darkness. When a thief comes to your house he only needs one door. He does not care if it is the front door, back door, or side door. Flies only need one open door to come into your house. Satan only needs one open door in your life. You need to close all the doors to the powers of darkness. What is the point of killing flies if a door is still open? You must first shut the door, and then start killing the flies. Partial repentance does not work because Satan will identify those unrepented sin areas in your life and will continue to "exploit and expand" his control over you. He is not stupid. Satan attacks you at the point of your vulnerability, not your strengths.

I often tell Christians that you measure your spiritual

strength based on the weakest area in your life. You might have a beautiful home surrounded by a ten-foot wall, but if there is a two-foot opening in the back, how protective is the wall? A chain is only as strong as its weakest link. Satan knows your weaknesses and he will continue to exploit those areas until you stand against the powers of darkness. This is accomplished by allowing the Holy Spirit to search your heart and repent of past sins and begin to shut the doors to the powers of darkness.

I would like to finish the story about John who was involved in the slave trade as a Christian with all its brutality and wickedness. Later the power of sin was broken in John's life. He then began working to have slavery abolished in England. He eventually testified before the Prime Minister of England on the brutality of the slave trade. England abolished slavery even before the United States. John became a minister of the Gospel and has touched millions of people. Perhaps you have heard about John or a famous song that he wrote. The song starts out: "Amazing Grace! How sweet the sound that saved a wretch like me!" The song is called Amazing Grace. His name is John Newton.

The grace that John is referring to is not just about salvation but also about God's grace in breaking the power of sin after salvation in a Christian's life. But this requires a choice and submission to God.

THE BATTLEGROUND

TWO SPIRITUAL KINGDOMS

There is a war going on in the spiritual realms between two very powerful kingdoms, the Kingdom of God and the Kingdom of Satan. The Kingdom of God is mentioned in the Gospel of John. "Jesus answered, 'My kingdom is not of this world. If My kingdom were of this world, then My servants would be fighting, so that I would not be handed over to the Jews; but as it is, My kingdom is not of this realm'" (John 18:36). The Kingdom of Satan is mentioned in the Gospel of Luke. "If Satan also is divided against himself, how will his kingdom stand?" (Luke 11:18). All people who have accepted God's offer of a pardon, that is, who have received Jesus Christ as their Lord and Savior, are part of the spiritual Kingdom of God. All other people who have never received Jesus Christ or have rejected him are part of the spiritual Kingdom of Satan. The people who are part of the spiritual Kingdom of Satan may even be religious, moral, and law-abiding citizens – that is not the issue. Being religious, moral, and law-abiding does not get you to Heaven. Accepting God's offer of a pardon does! A person is spiritually transferred from the Kingdom of Satan to the Kingdom of God when he receives Jesus Christ as his Lord and Savior. Thus, the salvation experience not only changes a person's relationship with God but also his relationship with Satan. "For He rescued us from the domain of darkness, and transferred us to the kingdom of His beloved Son" (Col. 1:13).

SATAN'S PHYSICAL KINGDOM

In this present age, Satan not only controls a spiritual kingdom but also a physical kingdom. It is undisputed that Jesus Christ is the creator of the world. "For by Him all things were created, both in the heavens and on earth, visible and invisible, whether thrones or dominions or rulers or authorities–all things have been created through Him and for Him" (Col. 1:16). Furthermore, Jesus Christ owns the entire world. "The earth is the Lord's, and all it contains, The world, and those who dwell in it" (Ps. 24:1). Although Scripture indicates that Jesus Christ created the world and owns the world, other verses seem to reveal that Satan has possession of the world and exercises limited authority over it. Thus, clarifying the difference between "ownership" and "possession" may provide some insight on the parameters of Satan's authority. For example, a tenant who rents an apartment has possession of the property; however, the landlord is the true owner. The tenant, since he has possession of the apartment, does exert a certain level of control over the property. The tenant can invite whom he wants to the apartment. In some instances, a tenant may even have the right to legally transfer temporary possession of the apartment to another person by a sublease. However, the tenant does not have legal title to the property.

Jesus Christ owns the world, but Satan has temporary possession of it. It appears that God granted possession or dominion of the world to Adam and Eve. However, when Adam and Eve sinned, they forfeited their right to legal possession of the world, and it was handed over to Satan. Jesus Christ has even implicitly acknowledged that Satan has legal possession of the world:

> "He [Satan] led Him up and showed Him all the kingdoms of the world in a moment of time. And the devil said to Him, 'I will give You all this domain and its glory; for it has been handed over to me, and I give it to whomever I wish. Therefore if You worship before me, it shall all be Yours'" (Luke 4:5-7).

In response to Satan's offer, Jesus Christ did not say, "Satan, I created and own this world and it is not yours to give away!" I suspect that Jesus Christ did not respond in this manner because He knew that Satan had temporary legal possession of the world and had the authority to transfer it to anyone he wished. Satan controls this world, to a limited degree, under the sovereignty of God. It is no wonder that Jesus Christ called Satan the "ruler of the world" (John 14:30). Furthermore, the visible presence of evil in the world such as war, crime, and violence, reveal that the world is subject to satanic power. "The whole world lies in the power of the evil one" (1 John 5:19).

Many believers fail to realize that the church of Jesus Christ is operating in the midst of the physical Kingdom of Satan. The true church of Jesus Christ comprises every person who has received Jesus Christ as Lord and Savior, regardless of denomination. The only way the church can operate effectively in the physical Kingdom of Satan is by the power of the Holy Spirit. Thus, if individual members of the church are not filled with the Holy Spirit, they are no different than soldiers in the middle of a battlefield with no ammunition. They could eventually become spiritual casualties as a result of attacks by Satan and his hosts. Thus, it is imperative that you are filled with the Holy Spirit. It is not enough to merely have the Holy Spirit residing in you. In the next chapter, I am going to discuss practical steps on how to be filled with the Holy Spirit. Yet, while living in the physical Kingdom of Satan, we can have confidence that God can keep us from the evil one. "I do not ask You to take them out of the world, but to keep them from the evil one" (John 17:15).

THE FLESH

While living in the physical Kingdom of Satan, the believer will be attacked by three enemies: the flesh, the world, and the Devil. The fiercest and most formidable enemy, the one which will give you the most trials in this life, is not the Devil, but is the flesh. The flesh does not merely refer to the actual human body but is a term describing man's capacity and desire to sin. Some temptations originate from the flesh, that is, from inside the believer. "Each one is tempted when he is carried away and enticed by his own lust" (Jam. 1:14). The flesh will never be removed while you are alive on earth and in your mortal body. Thus, you and I are the primary problem, not the Devil! I wish I could blame Satan and the demons for everything, but I cannot! Sadly, some individuals believe that after a person is born-again they lose the capacity to sin. Others believe that the flesh is removed at baptism. Both beliefs are false. The flesh cannot be removed, even by prayer, but it can be rendered inoperative so that you are not enslaved and controlled by your desire to sin. We will be discussing in very practical terms how this can be accomplished in Chapter 4.

THE WORLD

The second greatest enemy of the believer is the world. "You adulteresses, do you not know that friendship with the world is hostility toward God? Therefore whoever wishes to be a friend of the world makes himself an enemy of God" (Jam. 4:4). Exposure to worldly influences over time increases the probability that you will stumble and sin. You are exposed to worldly influences by what you listen to and by what you see. For example, having a constant diet of watching R-rated movies for entertainment where there are sexual scenes, violence, or cursing, will negatively impact your spiritual life. You may think that you are immune, but you are not. If you are serious about losing weight, you do not have two donuts for breakfast every day. Remember the old phrase "Garbage in – Garbage out." If you are serious about trying to obey Christ, cut out the garbage that is having a negative impact on your spiritual life. This garbage only increases the possibility that you will sin and open the doors to the powers of darkness in your life. "'Therefore, come out from their midst and be separate,' says the Lord. 'And do not touch what is unclean; and I will welcome you'" (2 Cor. 6:17).

When Scripture refers to being separate from the world,

I am not convinced it means to avoid all worldly influences. If that was the goal, we should all live in a secluded monastery and avoid all worldly influences so we might not be tempted with sin. Yet, it is not always a sin to be exposed to worldly influences. In many cases, it cannot be avoided. Being separate from the world also does not mean separation from lost people who are in the world. Remember, Jesus Christ and his disciples ate and drank with sinners. They even reached out to prostitutes. "The Son of Man came eating and drinking, and they say, 'Behold, a gluttonous man and a drunkard, a friend of tax collectors and sinners!'" (Matt. 11:19). Do you want to be like Jesus? Then you also must be friends with lost people. Too many believers have no friends who are lost. How are we to be salt and light and reach people for the Gospel if we do not have genuine friendships with lost people?

You must exercise caution in having close relationships with those who are not believers. Jude encouraged believers to reach out to lost people, to snatch them out of the fire of Hell, but at the same time he warned them to be careful. "Save others, snatching them out of the fire; and on some have mercy with fear, hating even the garment polluted by the flesh" (Jude 1:23). You also need to know your susceptibility, your weakness to temptations. You may want to spend time with a friend with the goal of ultimately sharing the Gospel. But you need to be careful that you do not become involved in his or her sinful activities. You may need to consider cutting off some relationships, at least temporarily, until you are spiritually stronger. You may need to take these measures if you are tempted to be pulled back into sinful activities. If a friend falls through the ice at a pond, your initial reaction might be to run out on the ice to help him. But if you are not trained on how to rescue someone who has fallen through the ice, you could fall in yourself and both of you could wind up dying. Instead, it might be best to call an emergency number or ask others around you for help. Having a good heart, but an empty head is dangerous. Yes, seek to develop relationships and friendships with lost people, but use wisdom in the process.

When Scripture refers to the world, it is also referring to the world's values that are contrary to God:

> "Do not love the world, nor the things in the world. If anyone loves the world, the love of the Father is not in him. For all that is in the world, the lust of the flesh and the lust of the eyes and the boastful pride of life, is not from the Father, but is from the world. The world is passing away, and also its lusts; but the one who does the will of God lives forever" (1 John 2:15-17).

The world's values can be put in three categories: First, love of money – wanting things. Second, desire for fame – seeking recognition and wanting to be the "rock star." Third, lust for power – wanting to be the "boss." These three things are what the majority of unsaved people seek to achieve. Christians often have these same worldly goals. They adopt the same values and try to justify them in their mind.

Love of Money

First, the love of money. How often have you heard someone say that they are asking God to bless them financially so they can give more to the church or missions? A very admirable goal. This could be true for some. But many, if they are honest, also want to be wealthy so they can buy more things. It all comes down to one issue—what is your real motive? As believers, we need to let God determine our standard of living and then ask God for contentment.

Desire for Fame

Second, the desire for fame. For example, a pastor might be praying to have a large church so he can have a greater impact on the community and reach more lost people for the Gospel. A very admirable goal. However, some pastors, if they are honest, also want the respect of being viewed as successful by their community and denominational circles. They want to be recognized. After all, it is the pastors of large churches who get invited to be conference speakers to show others how they became successful. Again, it all comes down to one issue—what is your real motive?

Lust for Power

Third, the lust for power. I was in the martial arts for many years. In many martial arts organizations, the highest-ranking black belt instructor runs the program like a military general. He has great authority over the students and those with lesser ranks. He is often spoken to with great deference. When he is approached by other martial artists, they will bow before him out of respect and honor. Many years ago, I read an article in a martial arts magazine where the author took the position that some individuals who have little or no authority over people at their job are often drawn to becoming high-ranking black belt instructors. In this way, they fulfill an inner desire of having power and authority over people. Of course, this may be true for some martial arts instructors, but certainly not all. Yet, this is no different in the church. Some Christians want to have leadership roles in the church. They say they want to serve the Lord. A very admirable goal. But some, if they are honest and search their hearts, may have mixed motives. Some perhaps, feel marginalized at their job or in life with little or no authority over people, but now as a leader in the church they are able to tell people what to do or are perceived as one of the "big shots." Again, it all comes down to one issue—what is your real motive?

If you are going to have victory in spiritual warfare, you really need to do some "soul searching" and evaluate how much of the world's values have crept into your life. One way to evaluate your heart is to ask yourself, "What do you daydream about?" God cannot use you to the extent that He wants when the world's values have crept into your life. They need to be rooted out. "Do not be conformed to this world, but be transformed by the renewing of your mind, so that you may prove what the will of God is, that which is good and acceptable and perfect" (Rom. 12:2).

THE DEVIL

The third enemy of the believer is the Devil and the demon spirits. They are the least of our enemies because when believers have successfully overcome the flesh and the world, they are less vulnerable to satanic infiltration. However, some temptations and spiritual bondages are demonic in nature. Unfortunately, many have an unbalanced viewpoint when it comes to the Devil and demon spirits. The first unbalanced viewpoint is that demon spirits are not real and therefore have no influence over people. Some contend that believing in demon spirits was merely a way for ignorant people thousands of years ago to explain pain, suffering, and why evil exists. They believe that in our modern society we now know there are psychological and medical issues that caused the problems attributed to demons in the Bible. This is a false and unbiblical viewpoint. The second unbalanced viewpoint is that every problem is a result of demon spirits. These people blame Satan and the demons for every sin they commit. They also believe that every psychological or health issue is directly caused by a demon spirit. This is also a false and unbiblical viewpoint. In reality, the truth is somewhere in the middle of these two extreme viewpoints.

The Bible clearly describes the reality of demon spirits. "For our struggle is not against flesh and blood, but against the rulers, against the powers, against the world forces of this darkness, against the spiritual forces of wickedness in the heavenly places" (Eph. 6:12). Jesus Christ recognized the reality of demon spirits. "When evening came, they brought to Him many who were demon-possessed; and He cast out the spirits with a word, and healed all who were ill" (Matt. 8:16). It is very important to understand that Jesus knew the difference between a physical illness such as epilepsy and a problem caused by a demon spirit. "The news about Him spread throughout all Syria; and they brought to Him all who were ill, those suffering with various diseases and pains, demoniacs, epileptics, paralytics; and He healed them" (Matt. 4:24). Here, Jesus healed those who had demons and those who had various physical illnesses.

The demonic realm is very real. Demons gain power over people by several ways including abuse, traumatic experiences, fear, and unrepented sin. Many people who are oppressed by demon spirits have, in the past, opened a door for them to operate by submitting to the flesh and allowing unrepented sin to exist in their life. The believer should not glorify Satan by attributing to him every spiritual problem, difficulty, or trial in his life. The believer must realize the power and consequence of his own sin. Often, unrepented sin in the believer's life, which is an open door, and not Satan, is the root cause of a spiritual bondage. Further, it is nothing but an excuse for the believer to blame the Devil when he sins since God has promised a way of escape for each temptation. We must accept full responsibility for our sin no matter how great the temptation. After a person is born into the Kingdom of God, victories in spiritual warfare begin with a proper understanding of the believer's three enemies.

THE FULLNESS OF THE HOLY SPIRIT

The early disciples needed to be filled with the Holy Spirit. It would have been impossible for them to carry out the Great Commission in their own strength. This is why Jesus Christ, after His resurrection, told the disciples to wait for the promise of the Holy Spirit before starting their ministry:

> "Gathering them together, He commanded them not to leave Jerusalem, but to wait for what the Father had promised, 'Which,' He said, 'you heard of from Me; for John baptized with water, but you shall be baptized with the Holy Spirit not many days from now'" (Acts 1:4-5).

You and I also need to be filled with the Holy Spirit. Specifically, we need the fullness of the Spirit to enable us to effectively witness. That is, explain to another person how he or she can be saved. This is the number one need of every person. We also need the fullness of the Holy Spirit to overcome temptation, conquer bad habits, tear down satanic strongholds, manifest the fruit of the Holy Spirit, and exercise the gifts of the Holy Spirit. However, the mere presence of the Holy Spirit in the believer's life does not guarantee that he is actually experiencing the fullness of the Holy Spirit.

EVERY TRUE BELIEVER HAS THE HOLY SPIRIT

The precise moment a person receives Jesus Christ as Lord and Savior, he or she receives the Holy Spirit. Some people have been taught that a person must seek after a second experience to receive the Holy Spirit. However, the Bible states that all who have received Jesus Christ have the Holy Spirit dwelling within them. "You are not in the flesh but in the Spirit, if indeed the Spirit of God dwells in you. But if anyone does not have the Spirit of Christ, he does not belong to Him" (Rom. 8:9). Yet, it is possible for the Holy Spirit to reside in the believer but not actually control him. When the Holy Spirit has only partial control of the believer's life, He often chooses to refrain from releasing spiritual power. It is similar to a battery in your car. You may have purchased a brand-new battery and put it in your car. But if there is a loose battery cable, the car will not start. The problem is not the battery. You do not need a new battery. Instead, you need to tighten the connection between the cable and the battery. In order to experience spiritual power, we must allow the Holy Spirit to have total control of our life. We must tighten our connection to the Holy Spirit by surrendering and committing every area of our life to Him.

THE HOLY SPIRIT WANTS ACCESS
TO EVERY AREA IN YOUR LIFE

The work of the Holy Spirit in the believer's life can be compared to remodeling a house. Scripture refers to the believer's body as a house. "We know that *if the earthly tent which is our house* is torn down, we have a building from God, a house not made with hands, eternal in the heavens" (2 Cor. 5:1, emphasis added). I find it very interesting that even the demons refer to the body as a house:

> "When the unclean spirit goes out of a man, it passes through waterless places seeking rest, and does not find *it*. Then it says, '*I will return to my house from which I came*'; and when it comes, it finds *it* unoccupied, swept, and put in order. Then it goes and takes along with it seven other spirits more wicked than itself, and they go in and live there; and the last state of that man becomes worse than the first" (Matt. 12:43-45, emphasis added).

I designed a small house. It has three bedrooms, two bathrooms, kitchen, dining room, living room, and a few closets. I want you to imagine that each room represents an area of your life. When a person is saved, the Holy Spirit enters your house. But that does not mean the Holy Spirit always has free access to every room. The Holy Spirit is a gentleman. The Holy Spirit wants to enter each room, but He will not force His way in. Thus, in order for the Holy Spirit to go into another room, He must be invited. When you ask God to fill you with the Holy Spirit, you are giving the Holy Spirit permission to go into every room of your house and clean up the messes and do some remodelling.

When a person is saved, the Holy Spirit enters him.

However, what often happens over time is that the Holy Spirit is forced to reside only in the back closet. This is because subsequent to salvation the believer refuses to surrender other areas of his life to God. The believer may also be resisting the Holy Spirit by allowing unrepented sin to exist in his life. While the Holy Spirit is forced to reside in the back closet, other rooms in the house get trashed, invaded, and occupied by the powers of darkness. This reminds me of what can happen when parents are on vacation and a teenage son or daughter decides to have an open party with a keg. People flock to the house and walk right in. The house gets trashed and the parents freak out when they return from vacation wondering, "How in the world did this happen?"

STEPS TO BE FILLED WITH THE HOLY SPIRIT

There are three steps to become filled with the Holy Spirit.

Repent of sin

Step one is to repent of all known sin. I previously discussed the difference between being forgiven of the penalty of sin and breaking the power of sin. I have already explained the need to repent of all known past sins as the Holy Spirit convicts you. I would refer you back to the principles we discussed in Chapter 1.

Surrender every area of your life

Step two to be filled with the Holy Spirit is to surrender every area of your life, every room in your house, to

God. This means everything. Let me explain what surrender means and what it does not mean. Surrendering an area to the Holy Spirit does not mean the area is already cleaned up and problem free. Instead, surrendering means you are willing to let the Holy Spirit come into that room to take charge and do some remodeling and clean up the messes. Thus, you need to determine what room in your life, what area in your life, is preventing you from being filled with the Holy Spirit.

I want to emphasize that the issue is not whether you are going to surrender a particular room to the Holy Spirit or keep it under your control. This is a false choice. Satan wants you to think that if you do not surrender it to God, you retain control yourself. Instead, each room in your life is either under the Lordship of Jesus Christ or the Lordship of Satan! There is no neutral territory. It is either one or the other. If you are afraid to surrender a room to God because you are afraid of what kind of "remodeling" God might do, think of the alternative. Remember, God cares about you; God wants to help you; God is for you; God loves you more than you love even your own children, nephews, or nieces. On the other hand, Satan hates you. Satan wants to destroy you. Satan wants to steal everything you have. Satan wants your life and family in ruins. Satan will have no mercy or pity on you. Do you really want a room or an area in your life to be controlled by that kind of person? Do you really want to have a room in your life that Satan and the powers of darkness have a legal right to invade, occupy, and destroy? And they will if you do not surrender it to God. Some of the areas you need to surrender to God include: past hurts, future dreams, goals, family, thoughts, time, church involvement, finances, offerings, material possessions, relationships, attitude toward spouse or parents, fears, tongue, self-esteem, pride, sexuality, health, eating habits, job, school, talents, gifts, and evangelistic opportunities. Keep in mind, there will be other areas the Holy Spirit will point out to you personally that will also need to be surrendered to God.

Claim the fullness of the Holy Spirit by faith

The third step to be filled with the Holy Spirit is to pray, in faith, that God would fill you with the Holy Spirit. Faith is merely believing God will do what He has already promised in His Word. Your prayer is an action step to implement belief. "With respect to the promise of God, he [Abraham] did not waver in unbelief but grew strong in faith, giving glory to God, and being fully assured that what God had promised, He was able also to perform." (Rom. 4:20-21).

By following all three steps, you are shutting the door of your house to Satan and opening the door to the Holy Spirit.

EMOTIONAL EXPERIENCES IN THE HOLY SPIRIT

The first time the believer becomes filled with the Holy Spirit may be a very memorable and emotional experience. However, we ask God in faith, based on His promise, to fill us with the Holy Spirit and we should not rely on our feelings. "For we walk by faith, not by sight" (2 Cor. 5:7). We all have different personalities and respond emotionally to events differently. For instance, I love going to Super Bowl parties. I can eat pizza and shrimp and quietly watch the game. There are other people who are yelling and hollering every time a touchdown is scored for their favorite team. It is fun to watch them get all emotionally exuberant. Yet, it is just how they are emotionally wired.

When a believer complies with all three steps and becomes filled with the Holy Spirit, it is not unusual for him to have an emotional response. Many will often experience a heaviness lifting, peace, joy, and confidence. In fact, often as the believer repents, surrenders, and asks God to fill him with the Holy Spirit, the darkness in him gets pushed out. Many people are delivered from demonic bondages when they become filled with the Holy Spirit. As the presence of the Holy Spirit comes into the room, as light comes into the room, the demons flee like a bunch of scared rats in a dark basement when a light is turned on!

When a person becomes filled with the Holy Spirit, he or she may discover their spiritual gifts. Upon being filled with the Holy Spirit, the supernatural gifts of the Holy Spirit are often energized that were previously given at salvation. Yet, it is important to understand that if the believer seeks the fullness of the Holy Spirit merely to have an emotional experience, speak in tongues, or to receive other spiritual gifts with prideful or selfish motives, he could be opening himself up to a demonic foothold or counterfeit. I want to emphasize there is nothing wrong with seeking spiritual gifts, even the more controversial ones, if done with the right motives and applying the truth of the Word of God.

THE FULLNESS OF THE HOLY SPIRIT IS NOT A ONE-TIME EXPERIENCE

The fullness of the Holy Spirit is not a one-time experience. "Do not get drunk with wine, for that is dissipation, but *be filled* with the Spirit" (Eph. 5:18, emphasis added). The translation of the Greek phrase "be filled," means to "keep on being filled constantly and continually."[3] People will often ask, "Have you received the Second Blessing?" My response is "Yes, but have you received the third and the fourth blessing?" This is because the believer must seek to be continually filled because he can lose the fullness of the Holy Spirit. A cup might be filled with water. However, if a small hole is created at the bottom, it will leak. Practically speaking, every time we willfully sin, we lose the fullness of the Holy Spirit. You cannot be filled with the Holy Spirit and filled with your selfish desires at the same time. Being filled with the Holy Spirit is like breathing. You inhale and exhale all day long. Being filled with the Holy Spirit is a continual process of repenting, surrendering areas of your life to God, and asking God to refill you with the Holy Spirit.

You also need to ask God to put His searchlight on your heart to show you new areas that need to be surrendered to the Holy Spirit. This is because the depth or level of the fullness of the Holy Spirit will vary based on your level of surrender to God. The believer should also continually reaffirm areas he or she has previously committed to God because it is easy to take those areas back. It is possible to slowly fade backwards spiritually.

EVIDENCE OF THE FULLNESS
OF THE HOLY SPIRIT

The Holy Spirit can manifest or give evidence of His fullness in many ways. At a trial, both sides present evidence to the judge, such as documents, pictures, or testimony. A judge should not decide the case based on the initial evidence but on the totality of the evidence. Similarly, in evaluating whether you are filled with the Holy Spirit, your primary focus should not be on the initial evidence but on the totality of the evidence.

Evidence of the fullness of the Holy Spirit includes the fruit of the Spirit and the gifts of the Spirit. One obvious evidence of the fullness of the Spirit is when a believer shares with others the good news of salvation through faith in Jesus Christ. A dear friend once said, "the Holy Spirit is for employment and not just enjoyment." The Holy Spirit wants to empower you so you can boldly, with wisdom, share the Gospel with others who desperately need to hear it. Remember, accepting God's offer of a pardon is the number one need of every person, whether he or she knows it or not.

A powerful evidence of the fullness of the Holy Spirit is transformation of the believer's life. It is a deep desire to obey God. It is the ability to progressively overcome sin. Did you know that God wants you to overcome? He does not want you to be like a caged gerbil on a wheel, always sinning in a particular area, feeling guilty but never overcoming. God wants you to overcome. God wants you to win. God wants to help you win. God wants you to be filled with the Holy Spirit, so you have the power to win. He wants the connection to the battery tightened so the car will start. However, it is your decision whether you are willing to take the necessary steps to be filled with the Holy Spirit.

4

OVERCOMING TEMPTATION

Sin is like rust or cancer that spreads to everything. Sin blocks the goodness of God and the power of the Holy Spirit. It blocks joy. It corrupts relationships. Unrepented sin is an open door to the powers of darkness to infiltrate your life. Hopefully you are working through the Sinventory (that I discussed in Chapter 1) and shutting the doors to the powers of darkness by repenting of your past sins as the Holy Spirit convicts you. However, you also need to plan to deal with future temptations. I am going to give some very practical steps to have victory in this area.

There are certain laws that govern the physical world. The Law of Gravity is one. If an object is dropped from a tall building, it falls to the ground instead of going up because of the Law of Gravity. As any scientist can attest, certain laws in the physical world are higher than other laws. For example, the Law of Aerodynamics can overcome the Law of Gravity. Thus, a Boeing 747 jumbo jet can take off from the ground based on the Law of Aerodynamics, even though the Law of Gravity seeks to prevent it.

THE LAW OF SIN

Just as there are laws that govern the physical world, there are laws that govern the spiritual world. One such law is called the Law of Sin. This law pulls the believer toward sin. The believer cannot overcome the Law of Sin by mere human effort or determination. The Law of Sin is so powerful that it can cause even a true born-again believer to constantly sin although he wishes to stop. The Apostle Paul referred to this law in the Book of Romans:

> "I know that nothing good dwells in me, that is, in my flesh; for the willing is present in me, but the doing of the good is not. *For the good that I want, I do not do; but I practice the very evil that I do not* want. But if I am doing the very thing I do not want, I am no longer the one doing it, but sin which dwells in me. I find then the principle that evil is present in me, the one who wants to do good. For I joyfully concur with the law of God in the inner man, but I see a different law in the members of my body, waging war against the law of my mind, and making me a prisoner of the *law of sin* which is in my members. Wretched man that I am! Who will set me free from the body of this death?" (Rom. 7:18-24, emphasis added).

Paul stated, "For the good that I want, I do not do; but I practice the very evil that I do not want" (v. 19). Evidently, Paul was completely aware of the power the Law of Sin had in his life and in the lives of other believers.

There is an important piece of equipment that allows your car to start. It is called a battery. If the cable is not securely connected to the battery, perhaps because there is corrosion or rust on the terminal posts, the car will not start. Imagine instead of driving your car to a grocery store you attempted to push it because it would not start. How far would you get? Some might be able to push a car for a block and others for only a few feet, but all of us would be exhausted. You would become very discouraged. You would eventually give up and quit. This is precisely what happens to Christians when they try to overcome the Law of Sin by mere human will power. It simply does not work. Many believers eventually quit trying and give up.

THE LAW OF THE SPIRIT

In the spiritual world, just as in the physical world, certain laws are higher than other laws. For instance, the Law of the Spirit is higher or greater than the Law of Sin. "For the law of the Spirit of life in Christ Jesus has set you free from the law of sin and of death" (Rom. 8:2). The Law of the Spirit can overcome the Law of Sin. As we previously discussed in Chapter 3, the Holy Spirit resides in every born-again believer. He is the greater power, the "battery", so the believer can have victory over temptation. However, the Law of the Spirit does not become operational until the believer surrenders every area in his life to the Holy Spirit. The believer must become filled with the Holy Spirit. Yet, even if you are filled with the Holy Spirit and have invited the Holy Spirit into every room of your house, there are additional principles that will help you to overcome temptation. Initially, you need to understand why people have a propensity to sin.

THE SIN NATURE

God created Adam and Eve perfect. However, after they sinned in the Garden of Eden, every one of their children, grandchildren, great grandchildren, great-great grandchildren, and down through the generations were born with a sin nature. "Behold, I was brought forth in iniquity, and in sin my mother conceived me" (Ps. 51:5); "Among them we too all formerly lived in the lusts of our flesh, indulging the desires of the flesh and of the mind, and were by nature children of wrath, even as the rest" (Eph. 2:3). In practical terms having a sin nature means that you were born with an inclination and propensity to sin. In fact, you may recall having struggled with a particular temptation or sin from your earliest days, even when you were six years old!

I had the opportunity to present the Gospel in the People's Republic of China. I was invited to speak at a clothing factory. The Catholic nuns had arranged for me to meet the owner of the factory and he invited me to speak in the evening to some of his employees. Also, various members of the Communist Party were present. After my presentation, the owner turned to the audience and asked if anyone had a question. One man, who was a medical doctor, told me that as communists they believe that their children are born perfect and do not have a sin nature. Of course, I could have opened the Bible and pointed out various verses that show every person is born with a sin nature. Instead, I merely asked the people in the audience how many of them had little children. I then pointed out that we must discipline our children even at age two and three. You do not need to teach a child to take a toy away from another child, hit another child, or disobey. They do these things naturally. Many of the parents in the audience smiled, acknowledging this is true. We discipline our children to correct these bad propensities. Although not conclusive, this is evidence that each child has a sin nature.

Several years ago, I took my family on a vacation to Orlando, Florida. When we entered one of the theme parks, they scanned everyone's thumbs for security purposes. This is because even though all our thumbs look the same, we each have unique thumbprints. Likewise, we all have a sin nature, but each person has a unique sin nature. The thumbprint of your sin nature is different than mine. In other words, your propensity to sin in a particular area from birth may be different than mine. We all struggle with a variety of temptations, but depending on the thumbprint of your sin nature, your struggle with resisting certain temptations may be significantly less or more than what other people experience.

A person may remember having a deep struggle with jealousy, anger, or a lack of self-control in eating, even in kindergarten. Not every struggle with a particular sin can be traced to bad circumstances or the environment in a person's life. The problem with some psychologists is that they do not acknowledge the possibility that a person is born with a sin nature. To the surprise of many, you may be struggling with a particular temptation, and it may not be the result of something you did earlier in life. It may also not be the result of something your parents did or failed to do. It may not be the poor environment that you were raised in. The real culprit behind your struggle with a particular temptation may be the thumbprint of your sin nature. However, do not go to the other extreme by justifying your constant criticalness, sexual addiction, or violent temper by merely saying, "God made me this way and other people should accept me the way I am." True, God created you, but you and I were born as fallen and broken people. You were born with a sin nature. However, God has stepped into this mess to redeem you, restore you, heal you, and give you a path to victory over temptation. Yet, I guarantee you it may be a struggle, one you can eventually win, but it will take a total commitment on your part.

THE NEW NATURE

My family and I have lived in a rural area for most of our lives. We have raised different kinds of animals. Pigs love a mud hole. If pigs are released near a mud hole, they will eventually wind up in it. They love to be in the mud. It is their nature to play around in a mud hole. Sheep are different. Sheep do not want to slop around in a mud hole but to graze in the pasture. This is their nature. It is possible for sheep to fall into a mud hole, but if they do, they will attempt to get right out.

Prior to salvation, a person had a sin nature. They had no choice but to be a slave of sin. This does not mean that a person prior to salvation could not overcome a particular sin or bad habit. However, the person's inclination and propensity were toward sin in general. He or she was in the "mud hole." Scripture teaches that a believer at salvation is given a "new nature" because of the indwelling Holy Spirit. "Therefore if anyone is in Christ, he is a new creature; the old things passed away; behold new things have come" (2 Cor. 5:17). The believer's new nature is to obey God. His or her inclination and propensity are now to obey God. There are times when believers may fall into the mud hole of sin because of the flesh; but because of their new nature, they will struggle to get out. In fact, a test to determine if a person has a new nature is to ask, "What is the deepest desire of your heart? Playing around in the "mud hole" of sin or obeying Jesus Christ?" When I am trying to determine whether a person is saved, I do not merely ask whether they recited a prayer to invite Jesus Christ into their heart. Instead, I ask, "Do you love the Lord Jesus Christ? Do you truly desire to obey God and keep His commandments?" This is the best evidence of whether a person is saved. After a person is saved and receives a new nature, sin can still dominate his life, but the believer now has the power to overcome temptation because of the indwelling Holy Spirit.

STEPS TO OVERCOME TEMPTATION

There are several important steps the believer can take to overcome temptation including recognizing your sin nature was crucified with Jesus Christ, considering yourself to be dead to sin, asking God to strengthen your will, and implementing the fundamentals.

Recognize your sin nature was crucified on the cross

The believer must recognize that he no longer needs to be a slave of sin. I am not saying that the believer, once saved, will never sin again. Instead, the believer does not need to be dominated and controlled by sin. It seems astounding, but Scripture reveals that the believer's sin nature was nailed and crucified with Jesus Christ on the cross. I do not understand how this occurred because I was not yet born when Jesus Christ died on the cross. Yet, I know that Scripture teaches that when Jesus died on the cross, God looked into my future and took all the sins that I would ever commit and placed those sins on Jesus Christ. God also took my sin nature and nailed it to the cross with Christ. This became a present reality for me at the time of my salvation. "Knowing this, that *our old self* was crucified with Him, in order that our body of sin might be done away with, so that we should no longer be slaves to sin" (Rom. 6:6, emphasis added). The believer must understand that the old self, that is, his sin nature was nailed and crucified on the cross with Jesus Christ. Due to this historical event, sin no longer needs to control the believer's life. Step one to overcome temptation is to thank and agree with God that your sin nature was crucified with Jesus Christ on the cross. "I have been crucified with Christ; and it is no longer I who live, but Christ lives in me; and the life which I now live in the flesh I live by faith in the Son of God who loved me and gave Himself up for me" (Gal. 2:20). The believer must reject the lie that he is powerless to resist sin.

Consider yourself dead to sin

Step two to overcoming temptation is to claim, in faith, that you are "dead to sin." Your fiercest and most formidable enemy, the one which will give you the most trials in this life is not the Devil but is your flesh. The flesh does not merely refer to the actual human body but is a term describing man's capacity and desire to sin. If you are a believer, even though your sin nature was crucified with Christ and you now have a new nature, you still have the capacity and desire to sin. I often refer to the flesh as the residue of the sin nature. In order for the believer to overcome temptation, he must put the flesh to death by the Holy Spirit's power. Or to express it in a different way, the believer must put the deeds of the body to death by the Spirit's power. "For if you are living according to the flesh, you must die, but if by the Spirit you are putting to death the deeds of the body, you will live" (Rom. 8:13).

My wife sews. Sometimes she inadvertently drops pins on the floor. Somehow those pins are drawn to my foot. There must be a magnet in my foot because no one else in our family besides me walks through the house and steps on the pins. I cannot tell you how many times a pin would get stuck in my foot, and it really hurts. I want you to imagine that you are at a funeral, and you stuck a pin in the hand of the dead person lying in the casket. There would be no response. He would not say "Ouch." This is because the person is dead to the pinprick. Likewise, the believer must claim he is "as a dead man" to the pinprick of temptation. The believer must claim, in faith, that he is "dead to sin." God then does His part and suppresses and deadens your desire to give into sinful thoughts that are presented to your mind. You do your part and then God does His part. "Even so consider yourselves to be *dead to sin*, but alive to God in Christ Jesus" (Rom. 6:11, emphasis added). "Therefore consider the members of your earthly body as dead to immorality, impurity, passion, evil desire, and greed, which amounts to idolatry" (Col. 3:5).

Ask God to reinforce your human will

Step three to overcome temptation is to ask God to give you supernatural strength in your will to reject sinful temptations. Believers cannot overcome temptation by merely deciding, in their own strength, that they will never sin. However, your will is still involved in the process. Rejection of sin is a necessary act of the human will. You are not merely a passive instrument. "Sin is crouching at the door; and its desire is for you, but you must master it." (Gen. 4:7). You must master sin. Your will is involved in this process. Your will is used when you thank and agree with God that your sin nature was crucified with Jesus Christ on the cross and you no longer need to be dominated and controlled by sin. Your will is used when you claim that you are "dead to sin." Your will is also used when you reject sinful thoughts that enter your mind.

Martin Luther once stated that you cannot stop the birds from flying over your head, but you can stop the birds from building a nest in your hair.[4] The same is true about temptation. Satan can place thoughts directly into your mind. You are not responsible for every thought that comes into your mind. Not every thought of hate, anger, lust, bitterness, or suicide originates from you. It could be the powers of darkness directing their fiery arrows into your mind. However, it does become your responsibility what you do with those thoughts after they enter your mind.

I often tell people to follow the "Two Second Rule." The rule is that you have one second to recognize an evil thought that comes into your mind and then you have one more second to reject it. If you reject it immediately, you have not sinned against God. However, if you begin to dwell on and play around with the thought, you just took the bait and now own it. You have just sinned against God and opened the doors to the powers of darkness. When an evil thought comes into your mind, I suggest that you pray, "Heavenly Father, I reject this thought of [i.e., fear, anger, lust, suicide, doubt]." Of course, these are just examples of some evil thoughts.

Only God can provide supernatural strength in the human will to successfully resist temptation. You must use your will to resist temptation, but your will is not sufficient, so God merges His will with your will. Thus, you need to ask God to reinforce your will with His will. The need for reinforcement is precisely why contractors use steel rebar in concrete. You need to ask God to put some steel rebar in your will. You need to pray that God would give you supernatural strength in your will to reject temptation.

You can implement all three steps to overcome temptation in a prayer to God when you are tempted:

> "Heavenly Father, I reject the lie that I have no power to resist temptation. I thank You that my sin nature was crucified with Jesus Christ on the cross and I no longer need to be controlled by sin."

> "I claim that I am dead to sin."

> "I pray that You will give me supernatural strength in my will to reject temptations."

Fundamentals to overcome temptation

Overcoming temptation also requires you to practice the fundamentals. The first fundamental is reading the Bible. You need to read at least one chapter from the Bible each day. The second fundamental is memorizing Bible verses targeting specific temptations. I will be providing suggested verses in Chapter 5 when I explain the Armor of God. The third fundamental is daily prayer.

The fourth fundamental to overcome temptation is fellowship with other believers. I attended a health club to lift weights. Bill, a member of the club, explained to me why he joined the health club. He said he is more motivated to lift weights with other people than merely lifting weights at home. Bill said that if he was lifting weights at home by himself, he might not train as hard, and after about ten minutes he might just quit and go lie on the couch. I admired his honesty. This is also one of the reasons why we attend church. It helps motivate us to serve the Lord. Also attending church is not just about what you "get out of it." The purpose of attending church is also being available to encourage and help someone else.

The fifth fundamental to overcome temptation is having an accountability partner. It is very important to have a spotter when using a bench press if you are lifting heavy weights. There have been people who have been killed while using a bench press. Their arms collapsed and the bar and weights came crashing down on their head. To prevent this tragedy, a spotter should be used. The spotter places his hands just under the bar so in case you cannot continue to lift the weights, he can grab the bar, so it does not fall on your head. A spotter could save your life. There is no embarrassment in using a spotter at a gym. It is kind of routine for guys and gals who are trying to push themselves. What does a spotter do? He motivates you. He pushes you to lift more than you think you can lift. He gives you confidence. You know that if your arms give out, he is right there to grab the bar. In fact, a good spotter may even yell at you and get in your face if you are not trying as hard as you should.

When you are struggling to overcome a particular temptation or you want to push yourself deeper into the fullness of the Holy Spirit, it is also helpful to have a spotter. Some call it an accountability partner. Actually, I do not like the term accountability partner because it has the connotation that only a weak and immature Christian needs to be accountable to another believer. I prefer to use the term spotter because a spotter pushes you to be your best to reach new levels in the Holy Spirit. Everyone needs a spotter if you are going to overcome temptation, become conformed to the image of Jesus Christ, and fulfill God's will for your life.

THE ARMOR OF GOD

"Finally, be strong in the Lord and in the strength of His might. Put on the full armor of God, so that you will be able to stand firm against the schemes of the devil. For our struggle is not against flesh and blood, but against the rulers, against the powers, against the world forces of this darkness, against the spiritual *forces* of wickedness in the heavenly *places*. Therefore, take up the full armor of God, so that you will be able to resist in the evil day, and having done everything, to stand firm. Stand firm therefore, HAVING GIRDED YOUR LOINS WITH TRUTH, and HAVING PUT ON THE BREASTPLATE OF RIGHTEOUSNESS, and having shod YOUR FEET WITH THE PREPARATION OF THE GOSPEL OF PEACE; in addition to all, taking up the shield of faith with which you will be able to extinguish all the flaming arrows of the evil *one*. And take THE HELMET OF SALVATION, and the sword of the Spirit, which is the word of God" (Eph. 6:10-18).

From about A.D. 60-62, the Apostle Paul was in a Roman prison. He had been preaching the Gospel. The Jewish religious leaders accused Paul of stirring up dissension among the people and desecrating the Temple, so they sought to put him to death. However, when a commander of the Roman Army examined him, he found that none of the accusations were deserving of death or imprisonment. When the Roman authorities were about to turn him over to be tried by the Jewish leaders, Paul exercised his right as a Roman citizen to have his case heard by the emperor.

While in prison waiting for his case to be heard, Paul wrote letters to various churches, including one located in the city of Ephesus. Toward the end of this letter, he described a spiritual war involving a vast army of spiritual beings also known as demon spirits. "For our struggle is not against flesh and blood, but against the rulers, against the powers, against the world forces of this darkness, against the spiritual forces of wickedness in the heavenly places" (Eph. 6:12). How is the believer to defend himself against such a powerful but unseen enemy? Paul answered that question by comparing each piece of a Roman soldier's armor to the spiritual armor of the believer. His selection of this analogy is not surprising. A Roman soldier was assigned to guard him during his imprisonment. Often Paul would be chained to the soldier. He had a lot of time to observe each piece of the soldier's armor and consider the spiritual analogies that apply in the believer's life. Paul was also undoubtedly aware of Isaiah's comparison of salvation and righteousness to pieces of a soldier's armor. (Isa. 59:17).

THE BELT OF TRUTH

The first piece of the Armor of God is the Belt of Truth. The Apostle Paul in Ephesians 6:14 instructs believers to stand firm "having girded your loins with truth" or having put on the Belt of Truth. The Roman soldiers wore a wide leather belt that protected the lower section of the body.

If the believer cannot discern the difference between truth and deception, Satan can neutralize his effectiveness in ministry. Satan is the father of lies. "Whenever he tells a lie, he speaks from his own *nature*, because he is a liar and the father of lies" (John 8:44). Thus, we need to ask God to reveal areas of deception in our lives. Deception can enter the believer's life when he has a misunderstanding of the Word of God. It is apparent that in the last days, many will be deceived in the area of doctrine. "For the time will come when they will not endure sound doctrine; but wanting to have their ears tickled, they will accumulate for themselves teachers in accordance to their own desires, and will turn away their ears from the truth and will turn aside to myths" (2 Tim. 4:3-4). No matter how much knowledge a believer has of the Bible and no matter how long he has been a Christian, he still can be deceived in the area of doctrine. The only way to be assured that your doctrine is accurate is to constantly read and study the Word of God. The Belt of Truth also protects the believer from four types of lies.

Lies about yourself

The Belt of Truth will protect against lies about yourself. We must confront deception and reject lies about ourselves. There are numerous lies that enter our minds. Some of the lies that many believers struggle with include:

> "You are not smart enough to study or understand the Bible."

"You will fail in all future business endeavors. You are such a failure!"

"You are not entitled to be loved by God and others. Who could love you?"

"You will never overcome certain sins or harmful habits."

"You will get cancer or some other disease" (when there is no rational basis to believe so).

"You have no ability to share the Gospel. Better yet, do not even attempt to share the Gospel because you will cause more harm than good."

"You are ugly, stupid, worthless, and no one would want to be your friend."

These lies and others must be broken to experience the fullness of God's peace and joy. You should pray, "Lord show me the lies that I have believed about myself."

Lies about other people

The Belt of Truth protects against lies about another person. Too often we misinterpret the words and actions of other people and draw false conclusions. This improper behavior is a barrier to developing healthy relationships. It can also produce unjustified bitterness or anger. Some of the common lies include:

Another person is angry with you – when she is not.

Your spouse has cheated on you – when he has not.

Another person is critical of your appearance and is judging you – when she is not.

Another person is prejudiced against you because of your race or financial status. He is looking down his nose at you – when he is not.

Another person has made a sexual advance toward you – when he did not.

Another person is full of pride – when she is not.

Your parents did not love you – when they did love you.

Lies about others affect friendships, family members, and ministry partners. Satan knows that you are spiritually vulnerable if you are isolated. Thus, Satan's goal is to place wedges in your relationships by planting lies to keep you isolated. You may believe a lie about another person, or you may be on the receiving end of a lie which is also very painful.

You may be correct in your perceptions of the other person in some instances. If this is true, you will still need God's grace. This is why we are to be patient with all people. We are not to take into account a wrong suffered. Yet, often the believer has merely accepted a lie and is speculating on how another person is thinking. You should pray, "Lord, show me the lies that I have believed about others and break the lies that others have believed about me."

Lies about God

The Belt of Truth also protects against lies about God. Here, Satan is trying to create a wedge in your relationship with God. In the Garden of Eden, God told Adam and Eve that if they ate from the forbidden fruit they would surely die:

> "The woman said to the serpent, 'From the fruit
> of the trees of the garden we may eat; but from
> the fruit of the tree which is in the middle of the
> garden, God has said, You shall not eat from it or
> touch it, or you will die.' The serpent said to the
> woman, 'You surely will not die! For God knows
> that in the day you eat from it your eyes will be
> opened, and you will be like God, knowing good
> and evil.'" (Gen. 3:2-5).

Satan tempted Adam and Eve to believe that God was a liar. Satan said, "You surely shall not die." Satan suggested that God was forbidding them to eat of the fruit to prevent them from being "like God." In other words, God was keeping something good and desirable from them.

Satan's lies often contain some truth. Adam and Eve did not immediately physically die, but they did immediately spiritually die and lost fellowship with God. Satan was accurate in stating their eyes would be open, but it resulted in shame and guilt. Adam and Eve now knew good and evil by personally experiencing sin; however, sin produced pain, sorrow, and ultimately their physical deaths.

Satan's strategy today has not changed. He continues to tempt Christians and others to believe lies about God. When Satan lies about God, he will often carefully add a small portion of truth for the appearance of validity. Some of the common lies that believers should reject include:

> "God will not forgive you of certain sins such
> as homosexuality, child abuse, rape, adultery,

murder, divorce, or incest." This is a lie. All of these sins are forgivable.

"God will only continue to love you if you refrain from sin."

"There will be no consequences if you sin against God because 'You are under grace.'" This is a lie. Remember, Satan adds a little truth to entice the believer to swallow the lie. It is true that the believer is under grace, but it is a lie that there will be no consequences if you sin against God and fail to repent.

"God is punishing you for your past sins whenever you get sick." This is a lie. Sickness can be discipline from the Lord for unrepented sin but not always.

"God cannot be trusted with your finances, employment, or health. You had better take care of yourself because God may drop the ball."

"God is mean spirited. If God is truly all powerful, but does not help you after you have prayed, it shows that He really does not care."

"All religions lead to God if a person is sincere in his beliefs."

"You have committed the sin of blasphemy against the Holy Spirit, the unforgiveable sin." Satan usually attempts to push this lie into the believer's mind at least one time during his or her lifetime. The Appendix contains additional information on what exactly is blasphemy against the Holy Spirit.

You should pray, "Lord, show me the lies that I have believed about you."

Lies about Satan

The Belt of Truth protects against lies about Satan. There are many Christians who claim to believe the Bible but reject some fundamental truths it reveals about Satan. The Christian cannot be effective in spiritual warfare if he or she has believed lies about Satan. Some of the common lies that Satan seeks Christians to accept include:

> "Satan does not exist but is a myth or merely a symbol of evil."

> "Demon spirits cannot develop a bondage in a believer's life, even if he or she indulges in habitual sin and fails to repent."

> "Hell does not exist or is not eternal."

> "Satan is more powerful than God."

> "Demonic bondages are always broken at the time of salvation." This is a lie. Sometimes demonic bondages are broken at the time of salvation but not always.

Accepting lies about Satan can weaken the believer's faith in God. You should pray, "Lord show me the lies that I have believed about Satan."

I own a Toyota Prius. It gets great gas mileage. In my opinion, one problem with the Prius is a blind spot on the left-hand side. When going into the left-hand lane, you cannot just look in your rearview mirror; instead, you must turn your head to look because of the blind spot. The four types of lies that I have just described are often blind spots.

You do not know they are lies because you believe they are true. If you knew they were lies you could reject them, but they are blind spots. Thus, you need to pray, "Lord, show me my blind spots."

THE BREASTPLATE OF RIGHTEOUSNESS

The second piece of the Armor of God that the Apostle Paul mentions in Ephesians 6:14 is the Breastplate of Righteousness. Paul may be referring to two types of righteousness: Gift of Righteousness and Practical Righteousness.

Gift of Righteousness

The Gift of Righteousness is described in the Book of Romans: "If by the transgression of the one, death reigned through the one, much more those who receive the abundance of grace and of the gift of righteousness will reign in life through the One, Jesus Christ" (Rom. 5:17). Jesus Christ is the only perfectly righteous person who ever existed. He lived a sinless life and found complete favor with God based on His own merit. A person is given the righteousness of Jesus Christ as a gift when he receives Jesus Christ as Lord and Savior. "If you confess with your mouth Jesus as Lord, and believe in your heart that God raised Him from the dead, you will be saved; for with the heart a person believes, *resulting in righteousness*, and with the mouth he confesses, resulting in salvation" (Rom. 10:9-10, emphasis added); "And may be found in Him, not having a righteousness of my own derived from *the* Law, but that which is through faith in Christ, the righteousness which *comes* from God on the basis of faith" (Phil. 3:9). After salvation, when God looks upon you, He no longer sees your sin. Instead, God sees the very righteousness of Jesus Christ.

Imagine a person who is unemployed, bankrupt, poor, and has no way to buy the necessities of life for himself or his family. He is in debt and owes $50,000.00. One day, a wealthy man, whose net worth is more than a billion dollars, learns of the person's desperate situation and is moved with compassion. The wealthy man then pays off the debt of $50,000.00. That alone would be enough for many of us to rejoice; having all your debts paid off! However, the wealthy man takes it one step further by signing an irrevocable document placing the poor person's name on all of his assets including financial accounts and real estate. Thus, the poor person now jointly owns all the wealthy man's property. His new riches are not based on his hard work or the money he has earned but the grace and mercy of the wealthy man.

There are two things that happen to you at salvation. First, your sin debt is forgiven. Second, God adds or credits to your account the very righteousness of Jesus Christ. Thus, when God looks upon you, He no longer sees a sinful and spiritually bankrupt person. Instead, God sees you in the very righteousness of Jesus Christ. In practical terms, this means that God views you as righteous as Jesus Christ. Once the gift of righteousness is received by faith, God will never remove it from the believer. The gift of righteousness is an eternal, unconditional, and irrevocable gift. "For the gifts and the calling of God are irrevocable" (Rom. 11:29).

Practical Righteousness

I love to eat pancakes. When making pancakes, you need to make sure both sides are golden brown. Do not make me a pancake with one side looking golden brown and the other side mushy. You need to flip it over and make sure the other side is also golden brown. We have discussed the gift of righteousness. Now we need to flip the pancake over. We need to discuss practical righteousness.

The Apostle Paul may also be referring to practical righteousness in Ephesians 6:14 when he instructs the believer to "put on the breastplate of righteousness." Practical righteousness is the performance of good deeds and turning away from sinful temptations. "For the grace of God has appeared, bringing salvation to all men, instructing us to deny ungodliness and worldly desires and to live sensibly, righteously and godly in the present age" (Titus 2:11-12). Practical righteousness should be the believer's goal after salvation; however, it does not achieve or maintain salvation. Practical righteousness is the natural result of salvation. When the believer sins, he must repent of those sins to God. "If we confess our sins, He is faithful and righteous to forgive us our sins and to cleanse us from all unrighteousness" (1 John 1:9). Salvation was given as a free gift, but it does not give the believer a license to sin. "For sin shall not be master over you, for you are not under law but under grace. What then? Shall we sin because we are not under law but under grace? May it never be!" (Rom. 6:14-15).

Sin always has consequences, even for a child of God. Sin does not sever a believer's relationship with God, but it does hinder his fellowship and communion. For instance, a believer with unrepented sin should not expect that God will answer his prayers. "Behold, the Lord's hand is not so short that it cannot save; nor His ear so dull that it cannot hear. But your iniquities have made a separation between you and your God, and your sins have hidden His face from you so that He does not hear" (Isa. 59:1-2). In my opinion, the number one reason Christians do not get their prayers answered is because of unrepented sin. It is as if you are trying to talk to God about that new job, a car, or some other issue, and God perhaps says, "I do not want to discuss that issue until we have first resolved your unrepented sin issue."

The presence of practical righteousness may also reveal whether a person is actually saved. "Little children, make sure no one deceives you; the one who practices righteousness is righteous, just as He is righteous; the one who practices sin is of the devil" (1 John 3:7-8). The Apostle Paul warned those who practiced sin:

> "Now the deeds of the flesh are evident, which are: immorality, impurity, sensuality, idolatry, sorcery, enmities, strife, jealousy, outbursts of anger, disputes, dissensions, factions, envying, drunkenness, carousing, and things like these, of which I forewarn you, just as I have forewarned you, that *those who practice such things will not inherit the kingdom of God*" (Gal. 5:19-21, emphasis added).

A person is deceived if he thinks he is going to Heaven merely because he recited a prayer, "Jesus come into my heart," when he continues to live in habitual and willful sin. These verses are the Holy Spirit's warning to us.

THE GOSPEL SHOES OF PEACE

The third piece of the Armor of God is the Gospel Shoes. The Apostle Paul in Ephesians 6:15 states, "having shod your feet with the preparation of the gospel of peace." When the believer is wearing the Gospel Shoes, he or she is prepared to share the message of salvation in any circumstance or situation the Holy Spirit would direct. Thus, the believer needs a basic understanding of the Gospel and be sensitive to share it whenever the Holy Spirit should lead. "Sanctify Christ as Lord in your hearts, always being ready to make a defense to everyone who asks you to give an account for the hope that is in you, yet with gentleness and reverence" (1 Pet. 3:15). Practically speaking, you need to have specific verses of Scripture memorized, or know where to find them quickly in the Bible to be able to explain the plan of salvation to a lost person. However, you do not need to memorize five hundred verses to share the Gospel. You need five. Five hundred is overwhelming. Five is feasible. The five verses you need to memorize are these:

1. Romans 3:23 explains that everyone has sinned.
2. Romans 6:23 explains that the penalty of sin is death.
3. John 3:16 explains that Jesus Christ paid the penalty.
4. Luke 13:5 explains that repentance of sin is required.
5. Ephesians 2:8 explains that faith is required.

While sharing the Gospel, you may be tempted with anxiety or fear. There will be times when we may need to pray for boldness and confidence in witnessing. Even the Apostle Paul requested prayer for boldness when sharing the Gospel. "Pray on my behalf, that utterance may be given to me in the opening of my mouth, to make known with boldness the mystery of the gospel" (Eph. 6:19).

Paul's statement, "having shod your feet with the preparation of the gospel of peace" could also be a reference to the type of boots the Roman soldiers wore. The soldiers wore boots that had cleats that dug into the ground so they would not slip in battle. There are two types of peace that can give believers a solid footing in spiritual warfare so they do not slip.

Peace with God

The first type of peace is "Peace <u>with</u> God." "Having been justified by faith, we have peace with God through our Lord Jesus Christ" (Rom. 5:1). The believer has peace with God because Jesus Christ has reconciled his relationship to God. Prior to salvation, we were enemies of God. Fortunately, God loves even His enemies. If you are saved, you are no longer an enemy of God. You have peace with God. The war between you and God is over. This means that when you close your eyes in death you can have peace because you are not an enemy of God. In fact, you are a friend of God. Thus, you will be welcomed and received by the Lord Jesus Christ and the holy angels.

Peace of God

The second type of peace is the "Peace <u>of</u> God." This type of peace gives the believer a solid footing in spiritual warfare. "These things I have spoken to you, so that in Me you may have peace. In the world you have tribulation, but take courage; I have overcome the world" (John 16:33). The indwelling Holy Spirit can give the believer the peace of God when turmoil and trials come into his life. It may

be a rational concern or an irrational fear. Thus, we need
to put on the Gospel Shoes of Peace when circumstances
come into our life that create fear, worry, and uncertainty.

THE SHIELD OF FAITH

The fourth piece of the Armor of God is the Shield of
Faith. The Apostle Paul in Ephesians 6:16 instructs believers to take up the "shield of faith with which you will be
able to extinguish all the flaming arrows of the evil one."
When Roman soldiers went out to battle, their enemies
would often shoot arrows at them that were dipped in tar
and lit on fire. To defend against this type of attack, the
soldiers would saturate their shields with water which were
made, in part, out of leather. This practice helped extinguish the flaming arrows. Likewise, the believer must be
saturated with the Word of God to extinguish the flaming arrows of the evil one. Your faith increases as you read,
meditate, and memorize the Word of God. "So faith comes
from hearing, and hearing by the word of Christ" (Rom.
10:17).

The flaming arrows of the evil one are the temptations,
lies, adverse circumstances of life, and doubts that are
directed at you by Satan. For instance, the evil one may
direct a thought of doubt into your mind that God cannot
be trusted. Faith is used to extinguish the flaming arrow
by having confidence and trust in the Word of God. This
means that you must know the promises of God. Some
biblical scholars suggest there are more than four thousand
promises in the Bible.[5] Again, you do not need to know
four thousand promises to be successful in spiritual warfare.

Try starting with four. There are four great promises in the Bible that may be helpful to you.

Promise 1 – God is with me

"Behold, I am with you and will keep you wherever you go, and will bring you back to this land; for I will not leave you until I have done what I have promised you." (Gen. 28:15).

Promise 2 – God will help me

"Do not fear, for I am with you; Do not anxiously look about you, for I am your God. I will strengthen you, surely I will help you, Surely I will uphold you with My righteous right hand" (Isa. 41:10).

Promise 3 – God will give me wisdom

"If any of you lacks wisdom, let him ask of God, who gives to all generously and without reproach, and it will be given to him" (Jam. 1:5).

Promise 4 – God will never desert me

"Make sure that your character is free from the love of money, being content with what you have; for He Himself has said, 'I will never desert you, nor will I ever forsake you'" (Heb. 13:5).

If you just know and claim these four promises, you can extinguish many of the flaming arrows of the evil one.

The Shield of Faith is also used when circumstances shatter your sense of control. Sometimes God allows difficulties to come into the believer's life and he or she may feel a lack of control accompanied by fear or uncertainty. The believer may be actively serving and obeying God only to find out that he or she has been diagnosed with a terminal liver disease, cancer, loss of job, financial ruin, or death of a child. Remember what happened to Job. When the believer raises the shield of faith, he or she is trusting that God is in control, even if the believer is not in control. "The Lord has established His throne in the heavens, and His sovereignty rules over all" (Ps. 103:19). The believer is trusting in God's sovereignty that nothing can come into his or her life apart from going through a divine filter. This does not mean that the believer will always understand why God has allowed the adverse circumstances.

THE HELMET OF SALVATION

The fifth piece of the Armor of God is the Helmet of Salvation. The Apostle Paul in Ephesians 6:17 instructs believers to "take the helmet of salvation." A Roman soldier would often face an enemy who used a double-edged sword which was about three to four feet long. The enemy would use this sword to try and decapitate or split the skull of the Roman soldier. The helmet, which protected the head, was absolutely necessary for survival.

The Book of Ephesians is a letter that Paul wrote to believers. He is not suggesting they need to get saved again when he says, "take up the helmet of salvation." Rather, Paul is emphasizing the importance of salvation. The believer has been saved – justification. The believer is being saved – sanctification. The believer will be saved – glorification. The Helmet of Salvation also protects the believer's assurance of salvation. The Bible states that you can know you have eternal life. "These things I have written to you who believe in the name of the Son of God, so that you may know you have eternal life" (1 John 5:13). Thus, the believer can have the assurance of salvation.

Some people experience continual doubts about whether they are genuinely saved. Concerns about salvation can either be warning signs from the Holy Spirit that you are not saved or doubts from Satan. In either case, the solution is to reflect on whether the Biblical requirements of salvation have been fulfilled. If the requirements have been fulfilled, the believer must stand in faith and exercise confidence in the Word of God. As I previously stated, the assurance of salvation is not the result of remembering a prayer that was recited a number of years ago. Assurance of salvation results from obedience. Obedience is not required to keep your salvation. Instead, obedience reveals whether you are truly saved. "By this we know that we have come to know Him, if we keep His commandments" (1 John 2:3).

THE SWORD OF THE SPIRIT

The sixth piece of the Armor of God is the Sword of the Spirit. The Apostle Paul in Ephesians 6:17 instructs believers to take the "sword of the Spirit, which is the word of God." The Roman soldiers used at least two types of swords. First was a long sword. The second was a short sword, more like a dagger. The Greek word for sword in Ephesians 6:17 is "machaira" and means the short sword, the dagger.[6] When Jesus Christ was tempted by Satan in the wilderness, he used the Word of God to neutralize the temptations:

"He [Satan] led Him [Jesus] to Jerusalem and

had Him stand on the pinnacle of the temple, and said to Him, 'If You are the Son of God, throw Yourself down from here; for it is written, He will command His angels concerning You to guard You, and, On their hands they will bear You up, So that You will not strike Your foot against a stone.' *And Jesus answered and said to him, 'It is said, You shall not put the Lord your God to the test'''* (Luke 4:9-12, emphasis added).

Jesus Christ responded to Satan's temptation by quoting Scripture. He actually quoted Deuteronomy 6:16. Believers also need to quote and rely on the Word of God when they are confronted with temptation. Practically, this requires more than merely understanding the broad principles or doctrines of the Word of God (long sword). Instead, you must memorize verses that target specific temptations (short sword – the dagger). Most believers will have limited success in overcoming certain temptations until they use the Word of God as a sword or a dagger, against the powers of darkness. King David discovered the secret to overcoming sin when he stated in Psalms 119:11, "Your word I have treasured in my heart, That I may not sin against You." The following are common temptations with suggested verses to use as a dagger against the powers of darkness:

Quarrelsome

> "The Lord's bond-servant must not be quarrelsome…" (2 Tim. 2:24).

Fear

> "When I am afraid, I will put my trust in You" (Ps. 56:3).

Revenge

> "Never take your own revenge…" (Rom. 12:19).

Sexual Lust

> "Now flee from youthful lusts…" (2 Tim. 2:22).

Swearing

> "Let no unwholesome word proceed from your mouth…" (Eph. 4:29).

Lying

> "Do not lie to one another…" (Col. 3:9).

Worry

> "Be anxious for nothing…" (Phil. 4:6).

Selfishness

> "Do nothing from selfishness…" (Phil. 2:3).

Grumbling

> "Do all things without grumbling…" (Phil. 2:14).

Vain imagination

> "Turn away my eyes from looking at vanity…" (Ps. 119:37).

Doubt

> "But he must ask in faith without any doubting…" (Jam. 1:6).

Unbelief

> "With respect to the promise of God, he did not waver in unbelief..." (Rom. 4:20).

HOLES IN THE ARMOR

The Armor of God is essential for spiritual warfare. Unrepented sin and deception can create holes in the armor. For instance, false doctrine or accepting lies about oneself, others, God, and Satan creates a hole in the Belt of Truth. Guilt can create a hole in the Breastplate of Righteousness when the believer fails to acknowledge the gift of righteousness he was given at salvation. When the believer is not prepared to witness or when turmoil and trials destroy his peace, a hole exists in the Gospel Shoes. When the believer doubts the Word of God, a hole exists in the Shield of Faith. When the believer has no assurance of his or her salvation, a hole exists in the Helmet of Salvation. When a hole exists in the Armor of God as a result of sin, repentance is the only way to repair it. When a hole exists as the result of deception, only applying the truth of the Word of God will plug it. You are vulnerable to demonic infiltration when there is a hole in the Armor of God.

THE HOLY ANGELS

CREATED BEINGS

There is so much mystery and excitement in the Bible regarding holy angels. Scripture provides a significant amount of information about the holy angels. The Bible declares that all things that are in the physical and spiritual realms were created by Jesus Christ:

> "He is the image of the invisible God, the first-born of all creation. For by Him all things were created, both in the heavens and on earth, visible and invisible, whether thrones or dominions or rulers or authorities–all things have been created through Him and for Him" (Col. 1:15-16).

The phrase "thrones, or dominions or rulers or authorities" is a reference to categories of angels, both holy and fallen. Thus, Jesus Christ is the creator of the holy angels. As created beings, the holy angels are not equal with God. Also, the holy angels are a separate and distinct form of creation. Humans do not become angels when they die.

TYPES OF ANGELS

There are various types of angels. The cherubim appear to be the highest rank of angel. Lucifer, who is later referred to as Satan after his fall, was the anointed cherub (Ezek. 28:14). Cherubim are extremely powerful and possibly have flaming swords. "So He drove the man out; and at the east of the garden of Eden He stationed the cherubim, and the flaming sword which turned every direction, to guard the way to the tree of life" (Gen. 3:24). It is conceivable that the holy angels use swords to battle demon spirits in the spiritual realms.

Another type of angel is the archangel. Michael is the only archangel mentioned by name in the Bible. "Michael the archangel, when he disputed with the devil and argued about the body of Moses, did not dare pronounce against him a railing judgment, but said, 'The Lord rebuke you'" (Jude 9). Notice that even Michael used caution when he communicated with Satan. He chose his words very carefully. His response to Satan when he disputed with him was merely, "The Lord rebuke you." In Chapter 13, I will be sharing more on the subject of communication with demon spirits.

Seraphim is another type of angel. Very little is known about this type of angel. The only reference to this particular type of angel is in the Book of Isaiah where they were praising God. "Seraphim stood above Him, each having six wings; with two he covered his face, and with two he covered his feet, and with two he flew. And one called out to another and said, 'Holy, Holy, Holy, is the Lord of hosts, the whole earth is full of His glory'" (Isa. 6:2-3). From this passage, we also learn that some angels have wings.

However, in other passages of the Bible, some angels are depicted as not having wings.

CHARACTERISTICS OF HOLY ANGELS

There are several interesting characteristics of holy angels. They are immortal. There was a beginning to their existence, but there will be no end. They will never die. In the Gospel of Luke, Jesus was discussing with His disciples what it will be like after believers are resurrected from the dead and are given glorified bodies. Jesus said believers will be similar to the angels who never die. "For they cannot even die anymore, because they are like angels, and are sons of God, being sons of the resurrection" (Luke 20:36).

Holy angels are emotional creatures. They have distinct personalities. Holy angels have similar characteristics with man, including a will and even emotions. "In the same way, I tell you, there is joy in the presence of the angels of God over one sinner who repents" (Luke 15:10). I find it very interesting that when a person receives Jesus Christ as their Lord and Savior, it causes the holy angels to rejoice. The fallen angels or demon spirits also have emotions; however, they do not display the emotion of joy. Instead, they often display the emotion of anxiety and fear (Jam. 2:19 and Luke 4:34).

THE NUMBER OF HOLY ANGELS

Holy angels are numerous. "Then I looked, and I heard the voice of many angels around the throne and the living creatures and the elders; and the number of them was myriads of myriads, and thousands of thousands" (Rev. 5:11).

The phrase "myriads of myriads" was used in ancient times if a person wanted to describe a vast number, *i.e.*, millions, billions, trillions, or even more.[7] It is the type of phrase used to describe the number of grains of sand that the universe could contain or the number of stars in the heavens.[8] The Bible often refers to angels as stars: "When the morning stars sang together and all the sons of God shouted for joy" (Job 38:7); "He counts the number of the stars; He gives names to all of them." (Ps. 147:4). If God compares angels to stars, could it be the holy angels are as numerous as the stars of heaven? Some scientists suggest there are seventy sextillion stars.[9] That is the number seventy followed by twenty-two zeros. If you took the grains of sand on every beach and desert in the world and then multiplied them by ten you would get about seventy sextillion. Thus, it is conceivable that the number of holy angels could be in the millions, billions, trillions, or even more.

THE POWER OF HOLY ANGELS

Holy angels are very powerful! In the Bible, two angels visited Lot. The men of the city tried to break down the door of Lot's home where the angels were staying. However, the angels had the ability to strike the men with blindness:

> "They pressed hard against Lot and came near to break the door. But the men reached out their hands and brought Lot into the house with them, and shut the door. They struck the men who were at the doorway of the house with blindness, both small and great, so that they wearied *themselves trying* to find the doorway" (Gen. 19:9-11).

After the angels struck the men with blindness, they destroyed the cities of Sodom and Gomorrah. The angels stated, "We are about to destroy this place, because their outcry has become so great before the LORD that the Lord has sent us to destroy it" (Gen. 19:13). The believer should never worry whether the holy angels are powerful enough to defeat a physical or spiritual foe. One angel had enough power to kill 185,000 soldiers when they sought to harm the people of God. "Then the angel of the Lord went out, and struck 185,000 in the camp of the Assyrians; and when men arose early in the morning, behold, all of these were dead" (Isa. 37:36).[10]

Although holy angels are powerful beings, the Bible indicates that eventually believers will have a higher rank than the angels. "What is man, that You remember him? Or the son of man, that You are concerned about him? You have made him for a little while lower than the angels" (Heb. 2:6-7). In the eternal state, the believer will have a higher rank, most likely because holy angels were never required to walk by faith. They walked by sight. They see the Most High in His full glory. The holy angels never experienced being born with a sin nature and struggling with the propensity to sin. They never personally experienced the pain of living in a fallen world that included disease and death. Yet, they watch and marvel at believers who walk by faith and love God even though they have never seen Him.

APPEARANCE OF HOLY ANGELS

Holy angels, generally, operate in the spiritual realms and do not have physical bodies. Holy angels are spiritual

beings and are invisible. "Are they not all ministering spirits, sent out to provide service for the sake of those who
will inherit salvation?" (Heb. 1:14). Daniel gives a dramatic
description of a holy angel who visited him:

> "I lifted my eyes and looked, and behold, there
> was a certain man dressed in linen, whose waist
> was girded with *a belt of* pure gold of Uphaz. His
> body also *was* like beryl, his face had the appear-
> ance of lightning, his eyes were like flaming
> torches, his arms and feet like the gleam of pol-
> ished bronze, and the sound of his words like the
> sound of a tumult." (Dan. 10:5-6).

Some have suggested that the appearance of the "man"
in Daniel Chapter 10 was the pre-incarnate Lord Jesus
Christ. This is because the description of this being is strik-
ingly similar to Jesus Christ's glorified body in Chapter 1
of the Book of Revelation. However, I do not believe this
being was Jesus Christ. We know by the context of this
passage that it was a holy angel. Later in verse 13, this being
states that a demon spirit over Persia had withstood him
for twenty-one days while trying to visit Daniel. Then
another angel, named Michael, had to come and help him.
In other words, the first being needed help because he was
blocked by a demon spirit. Thus, we know that the first
being was a holy angel because Jesus Christ would not have
needed this help.

Often when a holy angel appears there is dread and
fear. The Roman soldiers shook with fear when an angel
descended from Heaven and rolled away the stone from
the tomb. "Behold, a severe earthquake had occurred, for
an angel of the Lord descended from heaven and came and
rolled away the stone and sat upon it. And his appearance

was like lightning, and his clothing as white as snow. The guards shook for fear of him and became like dead men" (Matt. 28:2-4). Even when the prophet Daniel saw an angel he was frightened and fell on his face:

> "When I, Daniel, had seen the vision, I sought to understand it; and behold, standing before me was one who looked like a man. And I heard the voice of a man between *the banks of* Ulai, and he called out and said, 'Gabriel, give this *man* an understanding of the vision.' So he came near to where I was standing, and when he came I was frightened and fell on my face" (Dan. 8:15-17).

Holy angels, however, can mask their full glory and take on an appearance where they blend into humanity. The two angels who destroyed the cities of Sodom and Gomorrah had a human appearance:

> "Now the two angels came to Sodom in the evening as Lot was sitting in the gate of Sodom. When Lot saw *them*, he rose to meet them and bowed down *with his* face to the ground. And he said, 'Now behold, my lords, please turn aside into your servant's house, and spend the night,...' So they turned aside to him and entered his house; and he prepared a feast for them, and baked unleavened bread, and they ate" (Gen. 19:1-3).

There appears to be nothing about the angels' physical features that would have caused others to believe they were angels. True, Lot bowed down before them, but this may have been more of a recognition on his part that his visitors were servants of God. Most importantly, there is nothing in the passage that indicates Lot was in great fear like Daniel experienced when an angel appeared to him. In fact, Lot invites them to stay at his home and have dinner. There is a fascinating passage in the Book of Hebrews that states that some have entertained angels without knowing it. "Do not neglect to show hospitality to strangers, for by this some have entertained angels without knowing it" (Heb. 13:2). Holy angels are always surrounding believers. So, in a spiritual sense, we are always entertaining angels. However, this verse could also mean that some believers have literally entertained holy angels, perhaps had dinner with them or invited them into their home but did not know they were angels.

RESPONSIBILITIES OF HOLY ANGELS

Angels have a broad range of responsibilities. Holy angels deliver messages from God. This is seen in both the Old and New Testaments. For example, many know the familiar story of the angel Gabriel being sent by God to Mary to announce that she was going to give birth to our Lord:

> "In the sixth month the angel Gabriel was sent from God to a city in Galilee called Nazareth, to a virgin engaged to a man whose name was Joseph, of the descendants of David; and the virgin's name was Mary. And coming in, he said to her, 'Greetings, favored one! The Lord *is* with you'" (Luke 1:26-28).

Another part of an angel's job description is to offer praise and worship to God. After the angel announced the birth of Jesus to the shepherds, many angels appeared and were praising God:

> "Suddenly there appeared with the angel a multitude of the heavenly host praising God and saying, 'Glory to God in the highest, and on earth peace among men with whom He is pleased.' When the angels had gone away from them into heaven, the shepherds *began* saying to one another, 'Let us go straight to Bethlehem then, and see this thing that has happened which the Lord has made known to us'" (Luke 2:13-15).

Holy angels are God's servants who minister to believers. "Are they not all ministering spirits, sent out to render service for the sake of those who will inherit salvation?" (Heb. 1:14). This is a very fascinating passage because it states that angels "render service for the sake of those who *will* inherit salvation" (emphasis added). God does not exist in time. He sees the past, present, and future, all at the same time. God knows who will accept his offer of a pardon. It is not entirely clear, but this passage could mean that even before a person is saved, God is having the holy angels watch over them. The holy angels are perhaps aligning the circumstances in their life to bring them to the point of accepting Jesus Christ as their Lord and Savior. Regardless, this passage reveals that all believers have guardian angels who watch over them.

If you have accepted God's offer of a pardon, the angels will also serve you by ensuring that you are brought safely to Heaven. It is my firm conviction that the holy angels are with you at death and actually bring you to Heaven. "The poor man [Lazarus] died and was carried away by the angels to Abraham's bosom; and the rich man also died and was buried" (Luke 16:22). Abraham's bosom is an Old Testament metaphor for paradise or Heaven. This passage reveals that the angels carried Lazarus to paradise. Some people are afraid of death. They really do not know what to expect. Some fear that they will die alone. However, if you are a believer, you will never die alone because the holy angels will be with you when your soul is removed from your body. The holy angels will carry you to Heaven.

When a person dies who has never received Jesus Christ as Lord and Savior, some wonder if the holy angels or the demon spirits take the person's soul to Hell. The Bible does not directly answer this question. However, Satan does not have the keys to Hell. The Bible states that Jesus Christ has "the keys of death and of Hades." (Rev. 1:18). Hell is a place where God's wrath will be poured out on man for his rejection of God's offer of a pardon. The holy angels participate in executing the wrath of God:

> "The Lord Jesus will be revealed from heaven with His mighty angels in flaming fire, dealing out retribution to those who do not know God and to those who do not obey the gospel of our Lord Jesus. These will pay the penalty of eternal destruction, away from the presence of the Lord and from the glory of His power" (2 Thess. 1:7-9).

> "As the weeds are pulled up and burned in the fire, so it will be at the end of the age. The Son of Man will send out his angels, and they will weed out of his kingdom everything that causes sin and all who do evil. They will throw them into the blazing furnace, where there will be weeping and gnashing of teeth" (Matt. 13:40-42 NIV).

At the end of the age, it appears that it is the holy angels who actually throw unbelievers, those who have rejected God's offer of a pardon, into the Lake of Fire. It is very important to understand that the holy angels are not passive docile creatures. They execute God's wrath and judgment. They are greatly feared by the demons. We thank God for these character traits in spiritual warfare when we ask God to have the holy angels punish the demon spirits and take them to the pit when they attack us.

I am convinced that every believer has at least one guardian angel. "For He will give His angels charge concerning you, to guard you in all your ways" (Ps. 91:11). However, this does not mean that angels always protect the believer from physical dangers. Angels execute the sovereign plans and purposes of God. There are many situations where physical dangers come into the believer's life or their loved ones, and God directs the angels not to intervene. This is often hard to understand and is a mystery. "The secret things belong to the LORD our God, but the things revealed belong to us and to our sons forever" (Deut. 29:29). However, when we get to Heaven it will be explained to us how even the pain and hardships we experienced in this life were part of the sovereign plans of God and brought glory to His name.

There are always angels surrounding the believer. You will have great confidence in spiritual warfare when you understand the reality and protection of the holy angels. Holy angels stand between the believer and the powers of darkness. If the believer could see into the spiritual realms, he would see holy angels and chariots of fire surrounding him. When Elisha and his servant were surrounded by their enemies, Elisha prayed that God would open his servant's eyes to see the angels that were protecting them:

"When the attendant of the man of God had risen early and gone out, behold, an army with horses and chariots was circling the city. And his servant said to him, 'Alas, my master! What shall we do?' So he answered, 'Do not fear, for those who are with us are more than those who are with them.' Then Elisha prayed and said, 'O Lord, I pray, open his eyes that he may see.' *And the Lord opened the servant's eyes, and he saw; and behold, the mountain was full of horses and chariots of fire* all around Elisha" (2 Kings 6:15-17, emphasis added).

When God opened the eyes of Elisha's servant, he saw a multitude of holy angels surrounding them. The believer needs to see in faith what the servant of Elisha saw by sight.

It also appears that angels have a special ministry in guarding children. "See that you do not despise one of these little ones, for I say to you, that their angels in heaven continually see the face of My Father who is in heaven" (Matt. 18:10). I often wonder how many times God has directed the holy angels to protect my children, perhaps from a drunk driver or some other danger, and I was not even aware of it because no accident or harm occurred. In fact, it is only in a close call that we even think that God may have directed the holy angels to intervene. It is my conviction that when we get to Heaven God will reveal all of the times the holy angels intervened on our behalf. Perhaps this is why the Bible states that believers are going to judge the angels. "Do you not know that we will judge angels?" (1 Cor. 6:3). I believe this could also be a reference to believers participating in the judgment of the fallen angels who are now demon spirits.

The holy angels throughout the Old and New

Testaments protected the servants of God from evil. In the spiritual realms, the holy angels battle demon spirits who seek to hinder the plans and purposes of God. For example, in the Book of Daniel, the prince of the Kingdom of Persia was a demon spirit who sought to hinder a holy angel who was bringing a message to Daniel. There was a battle in the spiritual realms between the holy angels and the demon spirits for twenty-one days before the angel finally reached Daniel:

> "Then he said to me, 'Do not be afraid, Daniel, for from the first day that you set your heart on understanding *this* and on humbling yourself before your God, your words were heard, and I have come in response to your words. But the prince of the kingdom of Persia was withstanding me for twenty-one days; then behold, Michael, one of the chief princes, came to help me, for I had been left there with the kings of Persia" (Dan. 10:12-13).

After the angel gave the message to Daniel, the angel stated that he was now going to return to battle against the demon spirit over Persia and would also be battling the demon spirit over the country of Greece. "Then he said, 'Do you understand why I came to you? But I shall now return to fight against the prince of Persia; so I am going forth, and behold, the prince of Greece is about to come'" (Dan. 10:20).

In the New Testament, the angelic battles continue to occur. There is a constant battle between the holy angels and the demon spirits who seek to thwart the purposes of God. "There was war in heaven, Michael and his angels waging war with the dragon. The dragon and his angel waged war" (Rev. 12:7). Much of the warfare in the spiritual realms involve the holy angels seeking to prevent the demon spirits from harming man, both spiritually and physically. Jesus Christ, while on earth, stated that God the Father would have sent Him more than twelve legions of angels if He had merely asked for them. "Or do you think that I cannot appeal to My Father, and He will at once put at My disposal more than twelve legions of angels?" (Matt. 26:53). A legion consisted of six thousand troops.[11] Thus, Jesus Christ was stating that He could have asked God for more than 72,000 additional holy angels. It is my conviction that the Holy Spirit can prompt the believer to request additional holy angels when engaging in spiritual warfare.

THE BLOOD OF JESUS CHRIST

The blood of Jesus Christ is an effective weapon against Satan and his hosts. "They overcame him [Satan] because of the blood of the Lamb and because of the word of their testimony, and they did not love their life even when faced with death" (Rev. 12:11). This verse shows believers overcame Satan because of three reasons: the blood of the lamb, their testimony, and they did not love their life even when faced with death. All three reasons are vitally important, but I want to focus on the first reason these believers overcame Satan. They overcame Satan by the blood of Jesus Christ.

You may have heard a well-meaning Christian say, "If Satan attacks you just plead the blood." Some imply that it is almost like a silver bullet against the demons, that the phrase has supernatural power. However, the demons are not afraid of trite religious phrases or incantations that are used like a cliche and devoid of faith. "Pleading the blood" can be a very effective weapon against the demon spirits only when it is connected by faith to what it represents.

Thus, you must understand the purpose of the blood of Christ.

FORGIVENESS OF SIN (AT TIME OF SALVATION)

The primary purpose of the shed blood of Jesus Christ is that it allowed God to forgive man of his sin. Without the shedding of blood, there is no forgiveness. "According to the Law, *one may* almost *say*, all things are cleansed with blood, and without shedding of blood there is no forgiveness" (Heb. 9:22). The shedding of the blood of Jesus Christ released the believer from the penalty of sin. "Jesus Christ, the faithful witness, the firstborn of the dead, and the ruler of the kings of the earth. To Him who loves us and released us from our sins by His blood" (Rev. 1:5).

DELIVERS FROM GOD'S WRATH

The blood of Jesus Christ delivers believers from God's wrath and judgment. The final plague and judgment that God sent upon the Egyptians in the days of Moses is described in the Book of Exodus:

> "I will go through the land of Egypt on that night, and will strike down all the firstborn in the land of Egypt, both man and beast; and against all the gods of Egypt I will execute judgments—I am the LORD. The blood shall be a sign for you on the houses where you live; and when I see the blood I will pass over you, and no plague will befall you to destroy *you* when I strike the land of Egypt" (Exod. 12:12-13).

This event is known as the Passover. God stated that He would kill the first born of each household. This demonstration of God's power would convince Pharaoh to let the Children of Israel leave Egypt. However, God promised that He would pass over and not kill the first born of the Children of Israel if they followed a specific set of instructions. They had to slaughter a lamb and place its blood on the door of their house. By following these instructions, the Children of Israel demonstrated their faith in God that He would protect them. The Egyptian households that were not covered by the blood were not passed over and suffered the death of their first-born.

The blood of Jesus Christ applied to a person's life at the time of salvation delivers him or her from God's wrath and judgment. "Much more then, having now been justified by His blood, we shall be saved from the wrath of God through Him" (Rom. 5:9). God never changes. God is not a God of wrath in the Old Testament and then changed to be a God of love in the New Testament. God is a God of wrath and love in both the Old and New Testaments. "He who believes in the Son has eternal life; but he who does not obey the Son will not see life, but the wrath of God abides on him" (John 3:36). However, if you have accepted God's offer of a pardon, you are now covered with the blood of Jesus Christ, so God's wrath passes over you. Yet, God's wrath does not pass over the demon spirits. They are in the direct line of fire of God's wrath.

CLEANSES FROM SIN (POST SALVATION)

The blood of Jesus Christ cleanses the believer from sin that he commits after salvation. "If we walk in the Light as He Himself is in the Light, we have fellowship with one another, and the blood of Jesus His Son cleanses us from all sin" (1 John. 1:7). When a person receives Jesus Christ as his Lord and Savior, he is forgiven of the penalty of sin through the shed blood of Christ. After salvation, the believer can still experience sin. When the Holy Spirit convicts the believer of a specific sin, he needs to repent in order to be cleansed by the blood of Christ so that the power of sin will not dominate and control his life. The believer needs to experience a daily cleansing from sin. I assume that you wash your hands at least once a day. Likewise, you also need to experience a daily cleansing from sin so the power of sin will not take root in your life. "If we confess our sins, He is faithful and righteous to forgive us our sins and to cleanse us from all unrighteousness" (1 John 1:9). An example prayer of repentance for a sin committed after salvation would be:

> "God, I repent of [specific sin, *i.e.*, unforgive-ness, worry, lust, unbelief, anger, bitterness, etc.]. I turn from this sin. I thank you for the forgive-ness that I have because Jesus Christ shed His blood on the cross. Thank you for cleansing me from this sin. I shut the door to the powers of darkness in this area."

PROVIDES DIRECT ACCESS TO GOD

The blood of Jesus Christ gives the believer direct access to God. "Therefore, brethren, since we have confidence to enter the holy place by the blood of Jesus" (Heb. 10:19). In the Old Testament, a person did not have direct access to

God. The Temple in the Old Testament had three parts: the Outer Court, the Holy Place, and the Holy of Holies. There was a veil between the Holy Place and the Holy of Holies. Inside the Holy of Holies is where God communicated with Moses regarding the laws that would apply to Israel (Exod. 25:22). It is also where the High Priest would enter once a year. He would shed the blood of a goat for the Children of Israel. Then he would sprinkle the blood on the Mercy Seat which was the lid to the Ark of the Covenant. Everyone did not have access to the Holy of Holies to commune with God the way Moses and the High Priest experienced.

Today, believers have direct access to God because of the blood of Jesus Christ. This is why the veil that separated the Holy of Holies and the Holy Place was torn when Jesus Christ died on the cross. It revealed to the world that all people can have direct access to God. They no longer need to approach God through a high priest. Imagine if the president gave you his personal cell phone number and stated you could call him anytime day or night on any issue. Many would view you as a very powerful person merely because you had access to the president. Likewise, the believer has direct access to God because of the blood of Jesus Christ. The believer can discuss any issue with God, day or night. The believer can ask God to act and intervene in his life or in the lives of others. Many take their access to God for granted because they did not experience living in the Old Testament era when access to God was limited.

JESUS CHRIST PURCHASED THE BELIEVER WITH HIS BLOOD

The Bible states that Jesus Christ purchased the believer with His own blood. "Be on guard for yourselves and for all the flock, among which the Holy Spirit has made you overseers, to shepherd the church of God which He purchased with His own blood" (Acts 20:28). When you purchase something, it means you now own it. If you are a believer, Jesus Christ purchased you with His blood and now owns you. Jesus Christ owns you and all your material possessions. "Do you not know that your body is a temple of the Holy Spirit who is in you, whom you have from God, and that you are not your own? For you have been bought with a price: therefore glorify God in your body" (1 Cor. 6:19-20). Never forget that God owns all of your money and material possessions. You are just a steward responsible to manage God's property.

SEVERS OUR RELATIONSHIP WITH SATAN

The blood of Jesus Christ severed the believer's relationship with Satan. Sin separated man from God and caused Satan to claim everyone as part of his kingdom. When God purchased the believer by the blood of Jesus Christ, he or she was transferred from the Kingdom of Satan to the Kingdom of God. "For He rescued us from the domain of darkness, and *transferred us* to the kingdom of His beloved Son" (Col. 1:13, emphasis added). Now that the believer has been transferred to the Kingdom of God, his relationship with Satan has been severed. Satan no longer has any authority, right, or jurisdiction over the believer. Prior to salvation, the demons might claim a person's body as their house as discussed in Chapter 3. However, when a person receives Jesus Christ as his Lord and Savior, title to the "house" gets transferred and is under new ownership. You (the house) are now owned by God. It was paid for with the blood of Jesus Christ.

Imagine if you went to a closing to purchase your dream house, signed all of the paperwork, and were given the keys. However, when you went to your new home, you discovered the former owner was still living in the house and intended to stay. You would have a couple of options. Your first option might be to politely ask the former owner to leave, but he abrasively states that he will definitely not. He brags that he is bigger and tougher than you. He also has a volatile temper. You really do not like confrontation, so you decide to reach a compromise. You and your family will move in, but the former owner will be allowed to live in one of the bedrooms. This is not a good option but you compromise. The second option requires a bit of confrontation. You calmly remind him that you are the new owner of the house. It has been transferred to you. He is now a trespasser. If he is smart, he leaves at once. Blinded by arrogance, the former owner might continue to threaten you. However, if he does not immediately leave, you can call the police. When the police arrive, they will surround the home, drag the former owner out, and bring him to jail.

If you have accepted Jesus Christ as your Savior and Lord, your body (the house), is owned by God. You were transferred from the Kingdom of Satan to the Kingdom of God. Your relationship with Satan has been severed. The problem is that some demon spirits act as if they still own the house. They do not want to move out. They want to remain in a bedroom. Some Christians are simply not aware demon spirits are present. They may need to confront the demons and ask God to remove them from the "bedroom."

EFFECTIVELY PLEADING THE BLOOD OF JESUS CHRIST

Pleading the blood of Jesus Christ reminds the demon spirits they are merely trespassers, squatters, and must leave. It is a very effective weapon against them if it is connected by faith to what it represents. First, it represents that you have been forgiven of your sins. Second, it represents that God has purchased you and owns you. Third, it represents that your relationship with Satan has been severed. Many Christians fall into the trap of forgetting or not knowing the meaning and purpose of the blood of Christ. They use the phrase "pleading the blood" merely as an incantation, a superstitious, or magical phrase, which has absolutely no impact or power in the spiritual realms.

Pleading the blood will also have limited power when there is known unrepented sin in the believer's life. What would you think if a person claimed the protection of the blood of Jesus Christ while playing with a ouija board to contact evil spirits. Do you think that pleading the blood would protect them from the powers of darkness in that situation? I do not think so. I realize that this is an extreme example, but I am trying to make a point. To have confidence in the protection of the blood of Christ, the believer must have repented of all known sin. If there is any known unrepented sin, pleading the blood of Christ will be of limited protection against Satan. The primary purpose of the shedding of Jesus Christ's blood is for the forgiveness of sin. Yet, if the believer is in rebellion to God and not willing to repent of particular sins, he will not necessarily be protected from Satan, even if he claims the protection of the blood of Christ.

SATAN AND HIS FALLEN ANGELS

Satan is an actual spiritual being. The Bible describes Satan as having a heart and a will; these are personal attributes. Consequently, Satan is not a figment of the imagination, an evil influence, a mysterious force, or a synonym for evil. Instead, he is a spirit being who possesses many human attributes. Surprisingly, many people, including Christians, who say they believe the Bible, do not acknowledge that Satan is an actual spiritual being. You cannot fight against an enemy that you do not believe exists. It is important to understand Satan's origin.

SATAN'S REBELLION

"Son of man, take up a lamentation over the king of Tyre and say to him, 'Thus says the Lord GOD, You had the seal of perfection, full of wisdom and perfect in beauty. You were in Eden, the garden of God...You were the anointed cherub who covers, And I placed you *there*'" (Ezek. 28:12-14).

Chapter 28 of Ezekiel initially describes a person who is an earthly ruler or prince of Tyre. It also appears to be referring to a supernatural being. Thus, this passage refers to two separate individuals. In terms of biblical hermeneutics, which is a fancy word for the methodology of interpreting Scripture, this is called the "Principle of Double Reference."[12] This is where a single passage of Scripture applies primarily to a person or event near at hand (earthly ruler or prince of Tyre), but also applies to another person or event (Satan). There are several prophetic passages of Scripture that employ the Principle of Double Reference. One passage is in the Book of Hosea: "When *Israel* was a youth I loved him, and out of Egypt I called My son" (Hosea 11:1, emphasis added). The immediate context of this passage refers to Israel. Yet, it is also a prophetic passage referring to Jesus Christ:

> "So Joseph got up and took the Child [Jesus] and His mother while it was still night, and left for Egypt. He remained there until the death of Herod. *This was to fulfill what had been spoken by the Lord through the prophet*: 'OUT OF EGYPT I CALLED MY SON'" (Matt. 2:14-15, emphasis added).

Another example is in the Book of Deuteronomy: "The Lord your God will raise up for you a prophet like me from among you, from your countrymen, you shall listen to him" (Deut. 18:15). The passage is referring to Joshua. Moses is discussing his successor, Joshua, and that the Children of Israel must listen to him. However, the Apostle Peter, under the inspiration of the Holy Spirit, revealed that this is also a prophetic passage referring to Jesus Christ:

> "[Repent and turn] that He may send Jesus, *the Christ* appointed for you, whom heaven must receive until *the* period of restoration of all things about which God spoke by the mouth of His holy prophets from ancient time. Moses said, 'THE LORD GOD WILL RAISE UP FOR YOU A PROPHET LIKE ME FROM YOUR BRETHREN; TO HIM YOU SHALL GIVE HEED to everything He says to you'" (Acts 3:20-22, emphasis added).

In Hosea and Deuteronomy, the immediate context of the passages refers to Israel and Joshua, but they also have a broader meaning.

Satan was once a holy angel

The Bible provides definite clues that Ezekiel Chapter 28 is also referring to Satan. One of the clues is that it places this person in the Garden of Eden: "You were in Eden the garden of God…" (Ezek. 28:13). Who do we know that was in the Garden of Eden? Adam, Eve, God, and Satan! Ezekiel also describes this person as a cherub: "You were the anointed cherub…" (Ezek. 28:14). A cherub is a type of angel mentioned in the Bible. Satan was a cherub. He is referred to as "star of the morning" (Isa. 14:12) which is translated, Lucifer (KJV).

The Bible never states that Satan was the mightiest or greatest angel before he sinned. It does refer to him as "the anointed cherub." This does not necessarily mean he was the mightiest or greatest angel. If someone is a top lieutenant in the United States Army, we would not understand his level of responsibility or authority unless we also knew the entire hierarchy or chain of command in the Army. The Bible is a book of absolute and perfect knowledge, but it is not a book of total comprehensive knowledge. It does not provide a detailed description of the hierarchy and authority of each class of angels or whether there are other types of angels. Consequently, there is uncertainty whether Satan was the mightiest or greatest angel before he sinned. Nevertheless, as the anointed cherub, Satan had great authority and power in eternity past.

Satan sinned against God

> "You were blameless in your ways
> From the day you were created
> Until unrighteousness was found in you…
> And you sinned;
> Therefore I have cast you as profane
> From the mountain of God.
> And I have destroyed you, O covering cherub,
> From the midst of the stones of fire.
> *Your heart was lifted up because of your beauty;*
> You corrupted your wisdom by reason of your
> splendor"
> (Ezek. 28:15-17, emphasis added).

Lucifer (now known as Satan) was once a holy angel and was created with extraordinary beauty and wisdom. However, he sinned against God. Satan's sin was pride. "Your heart was lifted up because of your beauty; You corrupted your wisdom by reason of your splendor" (Ezek. 28:17). Logically, the fall of Lucifer must have occurred after God created the holy angels but before he tempted Adam and Eve in the Garden of Eden. However, Scripture does not pinpoint the actual time of his fall.

The Book of Isaiah provides additional details on Satan's fall. It appears that Satan led a rebellion against God:

> "How you have fallen from heaven, O star of the morning [Lucifer], son of the dawn! You have been cut down to the earth, You who have weakened the nations! But you said in your heart, 'I will ascend to heaven; I will raise my throne above the stars of God, and I will sit on the mount of assembly in the recesses of the north. I will ascend above the heights of the clouds; I will make myself like the Most High.' Nevertheless you will be thrust down to Sheol, to the recesses of the pit" (Isa. 14:12-15).

Isaiah's immediate subject of this passage is the king of Babylon (Isa. 14:4), but he is also referring to a supernatural being. This is another example of the "Principle of Double Reference." Here, Satan made several statements that indicated his desire to exist independent of God and to be like God.

Satan wanted to rule over the holy angels. Satan stated, "I will raise my throne above the stars of God" (Isa. 14:13). Satan is not referring to the stars that are in the physical world, instead he is referring to his authority relative to the holy angels. As we discussed in Chapter 6, the Bible refers to angels as stars: "When the morning stars sang together and all the sons of God shouted for joy?" (Job 38:7). In essence, Satan wanted to rule over all the holy angels.

Satan wanted God's glory. Satan stated, "I will ascend above the heights of the clouds" (Isa. 14:14). Satan is probably not referring to the clouds that are in the physical world. Instead, he is most likely referring to his ambition to have the glory and honor that belonged to God alone.

The Bible in several places refers to God's glory as a cloud: "It came about as Aaron spoke to the whole congregation of the sons of Israel, that they looked toward the wilderness, and behold, the glory of the Lord appeared in the cloud" (Exod. 16:10).

Satan's final statement sums up his purpose in his rebellion against God. Satan stated, "I will make myself like the Most High" (Isa. 14:14b). Apparently, Satan was not content with being the created one, worshipping and serving the Creator. Satan wanted to be God.

Satan deceived one-third of the holy angels

Satan succeeded in deceiving some of the holy angels to follow him. Some biblical scholars believe that Satan deceived one third of the holy angels to participate in the rebellion.[13] "His tail swept away a third of the stars of heaven, and threw them to the earth" (Rev. 12:4). Prior to the rebellion, Satan and the angels that followed him had a holy nature. However, after the rebellion, they surrendered their holy nature. They never again could experience the love, joy, and peace they had before the throne of God. There is no salvation for Satan and the angels that followed him in the rebellion.

Satan's rebellion failed

Satan's rebellion did not succeed. God stated, "You [Satan] will be thrust down to Sheol, to the recesses of the pit" (Isa. 14:15). After Satan sinned, he was not immediately imprisoned but was given a stay of execution. The final judgment of Satan and his fallen angels is that they will be eternally separated from God and thrown into the Lake of Fire. "The devil who deceived them was thrown into the lake of fire and brimstone, where the beast and the false prophet are also; and they will be tormented day and night forever and ever" (Rev. 20:10).

SATAN'S KNOWLEDGE

Before Satan sinned, God created him with incredible wisdom and knowledge. "Thus says the Lord God, 'You had the seal of perfection, full of wisdom and perfect in beauty'" (Ezek. 28:12). Obviously, Satan did not use his wisdom when he decided to rebel against God. However, when Satan sinned, he did not lose all of his knowledge and wisdom. Instead, these traits became corrupted by sin. Yet, the knowledge and wisdom that Satan and the demon spirits have is far beyond any human conception.

Although Satan has incredible knowledge, never think for a moment that he knows everything. Satan has limited knowledge and understanding—even in spiritual matters. There is also nothing in Scripture that expressly states that Satan can tell the future. I believe that Satan only knows about future events if God has revealed them to him. Satan is not omniscient (all-knowing). Even portions of the Bible are a mystery to Satan. He would not have sought to kill Jesus Christ if he had known that it was God's plan to resurrect him from the dead, bringing salvation to the world and sealing his own defeat. It is my conviction that Satan understands God's will in some situations only after the Holy Spirit has revealed it to the believer. It is conceivable that one of the reasons why God requires believers to walk by faith is to protect them from the powers of darkness. God rarely reveals all the future details of His will for your life. Perhaps if God did, Satan could more easily attempt to thwart them. Also, Satan and the demon spirits can accumulate and evaluate vast sums of data and may be amazingly accurate in some predictions. Therefore, the believer should never accept the source of an apparent prophecy or prediction as coming from God merely on the basis of its fulfilment.

I believe that Satan's knowledge enables him not only to understand the broad principles of the universe but also the minute details of an individual's life. For instance, Satan knows if you have accepted God's offer of a pardon. Satan knows if there is any unrepented sin in your life and an open door for him to work. Satan knows if there is any area in your life that has not been surrendered to Jesus Christ. It seems the believer is an open book to Satan. Satan and the demons literally know us better than we know ourselves. I believe that the demons are constantly conversing in the spiritual realms. They discuss the believer's strengths, weaknesses, and the best way to neutralize his or her effectiveness as a witness for the Lord Jesus Christ.

SATAN HAS BEEN DEFEATED AND DISARMED

Many Christians are afraid of Satan and the demon spirits because they do not understand that they are defeated. After Jesus Christ died on the cross, shed His blood to pay the penalty of sin, and was resurrected three days later, Satan was completely defeated and disarmed. "When He had disarmed the rulers and authorities, He made a public display of them, having triumphed over them through Him" (Col. 2:15). Satan and the demon spirits have not only been disarmed, but their defeat has been broadcast into the spiritual realms so that all of the holy angels are aware of their defeat. It is similar to the practice of the Roman Army after it conquered a nation. The Romans would strip the defeated army of their weapons and publicly humiliate them.

SATAN'S POWER

Although Satan is defeated and disarmed in his relationship to the believer, Satan still has tremendous authority and power in this age. He is referred to by the Holy Spirit as the "Ruler of the World." "I [Jesus] will not speak much more with you, for the ruler of the world is coming, and he has nothing in Me" (John 14:30). Satan is also referred to as the "god of this world." "In whose case the god of this world has blinded the minds of the unbelieving so that they might not see the light of the Gospel of the glory of Christ, who is the image of God" (2 Cor. 4:4). I have heard well-meaning Christians refer to Satan as a toothless lion. In other words, they claim that Satan can growl but cannot really bite or hurt you. This is false. The powers of darkness can hurt you. How many marriages has Satan destroyed? How many Christians has Satan tarnished their witness? How many Christians has he tempted to commit suicide? Yet, the believer must not forget that although Satan is powerful, God is all-powerful. Satan is mighty, but God is almighty. "You are from God, little children, and have overcome them; because greater is He who is in you than he who is in the world" (1 John 4:4).

It seems inconsistent to say Satan has been disarmed but that he can also harm the believer. However, these truths are not inconsistent. What would you think about someone who was confronted by an unarmed robber in their home. Fortunately, the homeowner happens to be carrying a gun. The robber begins to threaten the homeowner. The homeowner pulls out the gun, points it directly at the robber, and tells him to leave immediately. However, the robber begins to talk to the homeowner and convinces him to lower his gun. The robber then convinces the homeowner to give him the gun. The robber then points the gun directly at the homeowner and without hesitation shoots him. You may be thinking, "What a fool. That would never happen to me!" But this is precisely what happens to Christians every day in spiritual battles with the powers of darkness. Satan is disarmed. Thus, the only weapons that Satan can use to harm you are the weapons that you personally give him. Satan has a scheme or strategy to defeat the believer. "So that no advantage would be taken of us by Satan, for we are not ignorant of his schemes" (2 Cor. 2:11). Satan is disarmed, but he has a strategy to get rearmed.

Satan relies on three basic weapons to get rearmed that he can only acquire from the believer himself. The three weapons are the power of sin, deception, and the fear of persecution. Most of Satan's attacks against the believer can be placed in one of these three categories. We have previously discussed in Chapter 1 how Satan uses unrepented sin as an open door in your life. You prevent Satan from acquiring this weapon by repentance. We have also discussed in Chapter 5 how to protect yourself from deception by putting on the Belt of Truth which is one piece of the Armor of God. The third way Satan attacks the believer is through the fear of persecution. Christians in various parts of the world regularly face severe persecution. Some of this persecution is demonically instigated and inspired.

"Do not fear what you are about to suffer. Behold, the devil is about to cast some of you into prison, so that you will be tested, and you will have tribulation for ten days. Be faithful until death, and I will give you the crown of life" (Rev. 2:10).

I want to emphasize that Satan cannot lay one finger on the believer without obtaining God's permission. This is clearly taught in the Book of Job:

> "Then Satan answered the LORD, 'Does Job fear God for nothing? *Have You not made a hedge about him and his house and all that he has, on every side?* You have blessed the work of his hands, and his possessions have increased in the land. But put forth Your hand now and touch all that he has; he will surely curse You to Your face.' *Then the LORD said to Satan, 'Behold, all that he has is in your power, only do not put forth your hand on him.'* So Satan departed from the presence of the LORD" (Job 1:9-12, emphasis added).

Persecution comes in many forms. It can be verbal abuse, seizure of property, or even being put to death. Yet, we can be confident that God allows any persecution that comes into our lives. God is sovereign and has Satan on a leash. Any persecution that comes into the believer's life must first go through a divine filter in the same way that occurred with Job. However, the Church would be remiss if it is not training Christians to be prepared for persecution and to be willing to even surrender one's life for the Gospel. Suffering is the expected norm for the believer. "Just as it is written, 'For Your sake we are being put to death all day long; We were considered as sheep to be slaughtered.'" (Rom. 8:36). Our main goal as Christians should not be to maximize our number of years on the earth at any cost but to maximize our service to the Lord. Every believer must be willing to make the ultimate sacrifice of his or her life for the Gospel. There are millions of people all over the world who have never heard the Gospel. Many live in areas where there is severe persecution. Believers need to be fully surrendered to Jesus Christ and be willing to bring the Gospel anywhere on the earth that God would direct them.

Satan does not gain power over the believer through persecution. Instead, Satan gains power over the believer through the fear of persecution (the fear of man). This is a very important distinction. Fortunately, the Book of Revelation reveals how believers overcame Satan. "They overcame him [Satan] because of the blood of the Lamb and because of the word of their testimony, *and they did not love their life even when faced with death*" (Rev. 12:11, emphasis added). This verse reveals early believers overcame Satan because of three reasons. First, the blood of the Lamb. Second, their testimony. Third, they did not love their life even when faced with death. Many Christians focus on the first and second reasons these individuals overcame Satan but often ignore the third reason. Overcoming Satan requires us to love God more than even our own lives.

Absolute surrender to Jesus Christ removes the power and leverage of fear that Satan has over the believer regarding persecution. Jesus Christ told the rich young ruler in the Gospel of Matthew that he needed to sell his possessions and give to the poor. (Matt. 19:16-23). Jesus Christ may not be leading every believer to sell their possessions, but He is asking all believers to, at least, be willing to sell their possessions. Likewise, Jesus Christ may not be leading every believer to travel to a foreign country or risk their lives for the Gospel, but He is asking all believers to, at least, be willing to travel to a foreign country and sacrifice their lives. Believers should resist being manipulated by Satan with the fear of persecution. If believers fail to resist the enemy, they may not fully accomplish God's will for their lives. Remember, God's grace shows up at the time of our need, not ahead of time.

SATAN'S ORGANIZATION

Satan's kingdom is organized. Chapter 10 of the Book of Daniel provides a glimpse of the spiritual warfare that takes place between demon spirits and the holy angels over nations:

> "He said to me, 'Do not be afraid, Daniel, for from the first day that you set your heart on understanding *this* and on humbling yourself before your God, your words were heard, and I have come in response to your words. *But the prince of the kingdom of Persia was withstanding me for twenty-one days*; then behold, Michael, one of the chief princes, came to help me, for I had been left there with the kings of Persia'" (Dan. 10:12-13, emphasis added).

Daniel was informed by the archangel Michael that there was a demon spirit over the country of Persia. Later in this chapter, Daniel also mentions a demon spirit over the country of Greece (Dan. 10:20). This passage of Scripture provides evidence that Satan has an organizational structure. All armies need to be organized if they are to succeed in battle. For example, there are millions of men and women organized in the military, many at different levels of responsibility and rank. Could it be that Satan's kingdom is organized much like an army? We cannot be dogmatic on this matter, but it is not unreasonable to believe that Satan's organizational structure may include having demon spirits over world areas, nations, states, cities, false religions, and even individuals.

There is only one Devil whose name is Satan. As we discussed in Chapter 6, there are myriads upon myriads of holy angels. If biblical scholars are correct that one third of the holy angels fell in Satan's rebellion, the number of demon spirits could be millions, billions, trillions, or even more. A demon spirit is a fallen angel who functions as a worker of Satan. Satan is not omnipresent and cannot attack everyone in the world at the same time by himself. However, the way Satan has organized his kingdom allows him to attack everyone in the world simultaneously. Therefore, when the believer is tempted, it is probably not actually Satan who is directing the temptation in most situations. Instead, that temptation was probably delegated to a demon spirit who is assigned to the believer. Furthermore, there are some demon spirits who have more power than others. We know this because of Jesus' response when the disciples could not cast out a particular demon. Jesus Christ said, "But this kind does not go out except by prayer and fasting" (Matt. 17:21). Truly, our understanding of Satan's organizational structure is like looking at the tip of an iceberg. Even a believer with great spiritual insight and knowledge of Scripture can only understand or discern a very small portion of Satan's organization.

Finally, it is not the believer's knowledge of Satan's kingdom that gives victory but faith in the Lord Jesus Christ.

Know this, Satan and the demon spirits can never separate you from God's love. The Apostle Paul stated that nothing can separate the believer from God's love: "For I am convinced that neither death nor life, neither angels nor demons, neither the present nor the future, nor any powers, neither height nor depth, nor anything else in all creation, will be able to separate us from the love of God that is in Christ Jesus our Lord" (Rom. 8:38-39 NIV).

AUTHORITY OF THE BELIEVER

If a ten-year-old boy walked into a room and started ordering you to get out, how would you react? You certainly would not be intimidated. You might even laugh. The gall of a kid ordering an adult around! Let me change the facts slightly. What if that same ten-year-old boy walked into a room, and you noticed that he had a real gun in a holster. How would you react then? Everyone in the room would take notice. How would you react if that same boy then pointed the gun at a person in the room, pulled the trigger, and killed him? Everyone in the room would be frightened. What if that boy then pointed the gun directly at you and told you to get out of the room? You would be terrified. I suspect that you would get out of the room immediately. We all understand that a ten-year-old boy, by himself, is not a threat. However, a ten-year-old boy, with a loaded gun, who is willing to pull the trigger is a completely different story.

Even the most mature and spiritual Christian is like a ten-year old boy in the eyes of the demon spirits. But they are also aware that every believer is carrying a loaded gun and it is called the Authority of the Believer. Yet, the demon spirits know that most Christians do not even realize they have this weapon. Many Christians never take the gun out of the holster. The reality is that the demon spirits are absolutely terrified when a Christian learns about the Authority of the Believer and is willing to point it at the powers of darkness and pull the trigger by faith. The Authority of the Believer is one of the greatest weapons believers have against the powers of darkness. A basic understanding of the scriptural basis of this authority is imperative for every believer. I want to first explain Jesus Christ's authority in relationship to the powers of darkness.

JESUS CHRIST'S AUTHORITY OVER THE POWERS OF DARKNESS

Jesus Christ died on a cross for the sins of the world and His body was put in a tomb. On the third day, He was resurrected from the dead and ascended into Heaven. "So then, when the Lord Jesus had spoken to them, He was received up into heaven and sat down at the right hand of God" (Mark 16:19). After Jesus Christ's work on earth was completed, He sat down at the right hand of God. Jesus Christ is "seated" in a position of authority, not only above man and the holy angels, but also above Satan and the demon spirits:

> "These are in accordance with the working of the strength of His [God's] might which He brought about in Christ, when He raised Him from the dead and seated Him at His right hand in the heavenly *places, far above all rule and authority and power and dominion,* and every name that

is named, not only in this age but also in the one to come. And He put all things in subjection under His feet, and gave Him as head over all things to the church" (Eph. 1:19-22, emphasis added).

Jesus Christ is seated at the right hand of God "far above all rule and authority and power and dominion..." This language is describing the angelic and demonic hierarchy. Notice how Paul uses similar language in describing demonic powers in the Book of Ephesians: "For our struggle is not against flesh and blood, but against the rulers, against the powers, against the world forces of this darkness, against the spiritual forces of wickedness in the heavenly places" (Eph. 6:12).

BELIEVER'S AUTHORITY OVER THE POWERS OF DARKNESS

"You were dead in your trespasses and sins, in which you formerly walked according to the course of this world, according to the prince of the power of the air, of the spirit that is now working in the sons of disobedience... even when we were dead in our transgressions, made us alive together with Christ (by grace you have been saved), *and raised us up with Him, and seated us with Him in the heavenly places in Christ Jesus*" (Eph. 2:1-6, emphasis added).

The believer has authority over Satan and the demon spirits because he is "seated in Christ." The phrase "in Christ" is very important to conceptualize. It reveals an amazing truth about our relationship with Jesus Christ. It is obvious that the believer, while living on the earth, is not seated physically with Christ. Yet, the believer is spiritually "seated in Christ" who (in turn) is seated at the right hand of God in heavenly places. This is made possible by the Holy Spirit who resides in every person who has accepted God's offer of a pardon. The believer's unique relationship with the Father, the Son, and the Holy Spirit was brought to light in the Gospel of John: "In that day you shall know that I am in My Father, and you in Me, and I in you" (John 14:20). Remember, Satan and the demon spirits are subject to the authority of Jesus Christ. Satan and the demon spirits are also subject to the Authority of the Believer because the believer is "seated in Christ."

If you were appointed by the President to be an ambassador, say to Russia, you would go to Washington, D.C., presumably raise your right hand, and swear to uphold the laws and the Constitution of the United States. You would then travel to Russia. When the President authorizes you to make decisions in Russia on behalf of the United States, where is your authority based? Your authority is based "in Washington, D.C." and all of the United States backs you up including the President and the military. In the same way, when the believer engages in spiritual warfare against the powers of darkness and binds a demon spirit to the authority he has "in Christ," all of heaven enforces that command. It is enforced by the Father, the Son, the Holy Spirit, and the myriads of holy angels.

I was at an airport and noticed a police officer directing traffic. He could actually step in the middle of the street, raise his hand, and all the traffic would stop. The police officer had no power to physically stop the vehicles. Logically, a driver could just run over the police officer, but all the vehicles stopped when the officer simply raised his hand. This is because of who the police officer represents and his authority. Everyone knows that if you disobey a police officer, you not only have to contend with that particular officer, but with the entire police department and the judicial system. The officer has a radio and if you disobey the officer within a minute there could be ten officers surrounding you and they will arrest you. Plus, if you harm a police officer, I suspect they will make you an example and charge you with very serious crimes. You may be sent to prison for a very long time. So, when the police officer raises his hand and tells you to stop your vehicle, you make the wise decision to obey the officer. Likewise, Jesus Christ has given the believer authority over the powers of darkness. Jesus Christ has given the believer the keys of the kingdom of Heaven to be able to bind demon spirits. "I will give you the keys of the kingdom of heaven; and whatever you bind on earth shall be bound in heaven, and whatever you shall loose on earth shall be loosed in heaven" (Matt. 16:19).

TAKING AUTHORITY OVER TEMPTATIONS

The authority that Jesus Christ has given to the believer has many practical purposes including binding demon spirits who tempt the believer: "For this reason, when I could endure it no longer, I also sent to find out about your faith, for fear that the tempter might have tempted you, and our labor would be in vain" (1 Thess. 3:5). One of Satan's major activities is temptation. Satan cannot tempt everyone in the world at the same time. Satan is not omnipresent. This means that Satan, himself, is not present everywhere at the same time. Therefore, in the majority of cases, the temptations that come upon most believers are from demon spirits. Demon spirits can interject ideas and thoughts directly into the believer's mind. You must realize that a demon spirit can communicate with your mind. Every thought that you have is not necessarily your own. It becomes your thought when you dwell on it, then you own it.

If the believer discerns a spiritual being interjecting evil thoughts into his mind, he can take authority over the spirit and command it to leave. For example, the believer could pray:

> "Heavenly Father, I take my spiritual authority which I have as I am 'seated in Christ' at your right hand and I bind the demon spirit who is interjecting this thought of [*i.e.*, fear, worry, lust, suicide, doubt, etc.] into my mind. I command this demon spirit to leave."

You must proceed cautiously when deciding whether to bind a demon spirit because not all temptations are from demons. You must be sensitive to the Holy Spirit to know the source of the temptation. Frankly, sometimes it is difficult to discern the correct source. However, if a thought comes out of nowhere and does not follow a coherent thought pattern, it does at least raise a red flag. Yet, I also realize that thoughts in our sub-conscious mind can surface from the flesh into our conscious mind in an instant and may not be demonic. So, let me be clear. A temptation can have two sources. First, it can be a demon spirit directing an evil thought into your mind. Second, a temptation can originate from your own flesh. "Each one is tempted when he is carried away and enticed by his own lust" (Jam. 1:14).

Temptations from the flesh must be handled differently.

When a temptation originates from the believer's flesh, nothing will be accomplished by binding a demon spirit because the source of the temptation is not a demon. The source of the temptation is you. Instead, you must bring your flesh under the control of the Holy Spirit. The believer must consciously reject all sinful thoughts. You must take the thoughts captive using your own will through the power of the Holy Spirit. "We are destroying speculations and every lofty thing raised up against the knowledge of God, and we are taking every thought captive to the obedience of Christ" (2 Cor. 10:5). It is deception to blame Satan for every wicked thought that enters our mind. You must take personal responsibility for all thoughts that you dwell on. As I stated in Chapter 4, you could pray, "Heavenly Father, I reject this thought of [*i.e.*, fear, worry, lust, suicide, doubt, etc.]."

It is not a sin to have a wicked thought enter your mind but only when you dwell on it. So, reject the false guilt. Also, remember the two second rule that was previously discussed in Chapter 4. When an evil thought enters your mind, you have one second to acknowledge it. Then you have one second to reject it. If you play with the thought for more than two seconds, you now own it. If that happens, you then need to repent of the sin, or the door will remain open to the powers of darkness. Warfare in the spiritual realms often takes place in the mind. Until the believer has surrendered his or her mind to the Holy Spirit, he or she will have limited success in battling the wicked beings in the spiritual realms.

EFFECTIVE PRAYER FOR THE LOST

The Authority of the Believer can be used to effectively pray for a person to receive God's offer of a pardon. When praying for a person, the believer can request God to do several things.

First, the believer can pray that the lost person would hear and understand the Gospel. "How will they believe in Him whom they have not heard?" (Rom. 10:14).

Second, the believer can ask God to have the Scripture pierce the person's heart and have the Holy Spirit convict them. When I say convict, I mean a deep personal awareness, not merely an intellectual assent. You can pray the person would be convicted of sin. You can also pray that the person would have a deep personal awareness of God's holiness and righteousness. Finally, you can pray that the person would be convicted that there will be a day of judgment. "And He [the Holy Spirit], when He comes, will convict the world concerning sin and righteousness and judgment" (John 16:8).

Third, when praying for a person to accept God's offer of a pardon, you can also ask God to help the lost person believe the Gospel: "If you confess with your mouth Jesus as Lord, and believe in your heart that God raised Him from the dead, you will be saved" (Rom. 10:9). Some lost people have honest intellectual challenges in believing the Gospel. Through prayer, God can help a lost person resolve these issues.

Fourth, when praying for a person to accept God's offer of a pardon, the believer can also take authority over and bind the demon spirits who are blinding a person from understanding and seeing their need to receive Jesus Christ as Lord and Savior. "Even if our gospel is veiled, it is veiled to those who are perishing, in whose case the god of this world has blinded the minds of the unbelieving so that they might not see the light of the gospel of the glory of Christ, who is the image of God" (2 Cor. 4:3-4). It is clear from Scripture that Satan can hinder a person from understanding the Gospel and seeing their need for a Savior.

I had the opportunity to share the Gospel with a lady named Sheila. I explained to her the requirements to receive Jesus Christ. She knew she was a sinner. She knew that the penalty of sin was eternal punishment. She believed that Jesus Christ died on the cross, shed His blood for her sin, and was resurrected from the dead. I then told her about the requirement to repent of sin. As I discussed the need for repentance, she said that point makes her afraid. I asked her what she was afraid of. She really could not explain the fear. It appeared to be an irrational fear. This sent up a red flag to me. I thought that perhaps the powers of darkness may be behind the fear and were hindering her from receiving Christ. I asked if I could pray for her. She agreed. In my prayer, I took my authority in Christ and bound all of the powers of darkness which were causing this fear. After praying, I again explained about the requirement of repentance. This time she expressed no fear. About ten minutes later, she prayed with tears to receive Jesus Christ as her Lord and Savior. Thus, in some cases the believer needs to bind the demon spirits who are hindering a person from receiving Jesus Christ. For example, you could pray:

> "Heavenly Father, I take my spiritual authority which I have as I am 'seated in Christ' at your right hand, and I bind the demon spirits who are blinding and hindering [Name of Person] from

understanding the Gospel and seeing his need to receive Jesus Christ as Lord and Savior."

Finally, the Authority of the Believer can also be used to bind demon spirits who seek to steal the Word of God. Satan can steal the Word of God when it is preached to hinder a person from receiving Jesus Christ as Lord and Savior. "When anyone hears the word of the kingdom and does not understand it, the evil one comes and snatches away what has been sown in his heart" (Matt. 13:19). For instance, if a church is having a meeting where a message is going to be preached on salvation, there are demon spirits present who will try to prevent the Word of God from taking root in a lost person's heart. Thus, the believer could pray:

> "Heavenly Father, I take my spiritual authority which I have as I am 'seated in Christ' at your right hand, and I bind the demon spirits who will try to steal the Word of God from people's hearts and minds to hinder them from receiving Jesus Christ as Lord and Savior."

The Authority of the Believer is an important weapon of warfare in evangelism.

DEMONIC OPPOSITION TO MINISTRY

The Authority of the Believer can also be used to bind demon spirits when they endeavor to thwart a ministry. For instance, Satan will often oppose believers starting a new church, teaching a Bible study, starting a discipleship program, or reaching out to the community through evangelism. Satan and the demon spirits will oppose and attack any ministry that is in the will of God. Many ministries have failed because Satan thwarted them. Satan thwarted the Apostle Paul when he wanted to personally minister at a church in Thessalonica. "We wanted to come to you–I, Paul, more than once–and yet Satan thwarted us" (1 Thess. 2:18).

If Satan is not opposed in spiritual battle through prayer, he will often prevail in destroying a ministry. It was God's will to give the Children of Israel the Promised Land. However, they had to battle and defeat some very powerful enemies. God did not give the Children of Israel the Promised Land on a silver platter. In the same way, Satan and the demon spirits may need to be confronted and defeated in spiritual warfare to prevent them from thwarting a ministry. The Authority of the Believer is an important weapon that should be used in protecting and establishing any ministry. For example, if a new church is being established, the believer might pray:

> "Heavenly Father, I take my spiritual authority which I have as I am 'seated in Christ' at your right hand and I bind the demon spirits who are trying to thwart and prevent this ministry from being established."

Ineffective ministries are not always the result of a direct demonic attack. It could be unrepented sin in the life of the leaders or the congregation. It could be a lack of prayer. Many believers give lip service to prayer. They really do not believe it works. It could also be that the particular ministry is not in the will of God. For example, God's will was revealed to Paul that he should not preach the Gospel in Asia: "They passed through the Phrygian and Galatian region, having been forbidden by the Holy Spirit to speak the word in Asia" (Acts 16:6). Apparently, God had a timing issue regarding when Paul was to preach in Asia. I suspect that if Paul had gone ahead to Asia immediately, thinking in his flesh, "these people also need to hear the Gospel," his ministry would have failed, been ineffective, and produced little fruit. It would have failed, not because Satan thwarted it, but because Paul would not have been in the will of God ministering in Asia at that particular time. By the way, God later opened the door for the people to hear the Gospel in Asia. We also need to trust God's time-table in ministry opportunities.

REMOVING DEMON SPIRITS

The Authority of the Believer can also be used to remove a demon spirit and break a bondage in your life or in the life of another person. Demon spirits can influence a person from the outside and they can also dwell inside a person. Jesus Christ has given the believer authority to command a demon spirit to leave:

> "It happened that as we were going to the place of prayer, a slave-girl having a spirit of divination met us, who was bringing her masters much profit by fortune-telling. Following after Paul and us, she kept crying out, saying, 'These men are bond-servants of the Most High God, who are proclaiming to you the way of salvation.' She continued doing this for many days. *But Paul was greatly annoyed, and turned and said to the spirit, 'I command you in the name of Jesus Christ to come out of her!'* And it came out at that very moment" (Acts 16:16-18, emphasis added).

There is a spiritual gift called "distinguishing of spirits" (1 Cor. 12:10). This spiritual gift may be helpful in determining if a person has a demonic bondage. However, it is important to understand that the ability to remove a demon spirit or break a demonic bondage is not a spiritual gift. Instead, it is based on the authority all believers have as they are "seated in Christ."

> "Behold, I have given you authority to tread on serpents and scorpions, and over all the power of the enemy, and nothing will injure you. *Nevertheless do not rejoice in this, that the spirits are subject to you*, but rejoice that your names are recorded in heaven" (Luke 10:19-20, emphasis added).

If the powers of darkness have created a spiritual bondage in your life, either through unrepented sin (and you have now repented of those sins) or deception (and you have now rejected those lies), the next step is to use the Authority of the Believer to break that spiritual bondage. You need to pull the trigger. For example, you might pray:

> "Heavenly Father, I have repented of [specific sin, *i.e.*, unforgiveness, worry, lust, unbelief, anger, bitterness, etc.]. I have shut the door to the powers of darkness in my life. I now take my spiritual authority which I have as I am 'seated in Christ' at your right hand and I bind the demon spirits who have created this spiritual bondage in my life, and I command them to leave me and go to the pit."

There is an important point to remember. Some bondages are broken immediately, and others are broken over time. So do not be discouraged if the bondage is not broken immediately, but continue to stand firm against the powers of darkness commanding them to leave, claiming the promises of the Word of God and being diligent in prayer.

It is absolutely foolish to confront a demon spirit in another person without understanding and using the Authority of the Believer. In the Book of Acts, there is an account of a group of men who confronted an evil spirit in their own power and the tragedy that resulted:

> "Some of the Jewish exorcists, who went from place to place, attempted to name over those who had the evil spirits the name of the Lord Jesus, saying, 'I adjure you by Jesus whom Paul preaches.' Seven sons of one Sceva, a Jewish chief priest, were doing this. And the evil spirit answered and said to them, 'I recognize Jesus, and I know about Paul, but who are you?' And the man, in whom was the evil spirit, leaped on them and subdued all of them and overpowered them, so that they fled out of that house naked and wounded" (Acts 19:13-16).

Believers, on the other hand, do not need to fear demon spirits when they confront them in another person with their authority "in Christ." If you understand and use the Authority of the Believer, the demons know who you are, they know your name, and they fear you.

In the majority of cases, when you command a demon to leave or to break a demonic bondage in another person, there is no visible or outward manifestation. The person will feel nothing, except perhaps that a heaviness has been lifted. In a small number of cases, a demon spirit might communicate using the vocal cords of the person they indwell (*i.e.*, Luke 8:26-31). Sometimes the demons will make threatening remarks to the believer who is seeking to take authority over them and commanding them to leave. The believer should not yield to the fear the demons try to induce. They are often just testing you and bluffing. The demons are more afraid of you than you will ever be of them. You have the gun, the Authority of the Believer – and they know it! They are terrified of the believer who is willing to use his authority "in Christ" and pull the trigger. The demons also realize that Jesus Christ defeated and disarmed them at the cross through the shedding of His blood. As I stated in Chapter 8, the demons realize that they have no power over you, except through unrepented sin, deception, and the fear of persecution. The demons realize that they cannot touch you except by God's permission. Even Satan had to ask God's permission to afflict Job and sift Peter. The demons also realize that the holy angels are right beside you to enforce your commands and protect you. Finally, the demon spirits realize that the believer has the authority to send them to the pit.

AUTHORITY TO SEND THE DEMONS TO THE PIT

The Lake of Fire was originally created for Satan and the demon spirits. One day, they will all be thrown into the Lake of Fire. This will be their final judgment. "He [Jesus Christ] will also say to those on His left, 'Depart from Me, accursed ones, into the eternal fire which has been prepared for the devil and his angels" (Matt. 25:41). After Satan and his angels sinned against God in the rebellion, God created a place known as the bottomless pit, also known as the abyss, or Hell. This appears to be a temporary holding place for the demons until the final judgment. The terms "the bottomless pit" and "the abyss" are often used interchangeably or in the same context (*i.e.*, Rev. 9:1 and Luke 8:31).

There are demon spirits currently imprisoned in the pit. Some of the angels who participated in Satan's rebellion against God, were immediately cast into the pit, while others were allowed to inhabit the earth. "For if God did not spare angels when they sinned, but cast them into hell and committed them to pits of darkness, reserved for judgment…" (2 Pet. 2:4). We are not sure why some of the fallen angels were immediately confined after the rebellion and others were not. I also believe that some of the demons who participated in the evil that was perpetrated on the earth prior to the flood as described in Chapter 6 of Genesis are also imprisoned in the pit. There is also a reasonable basis to believe that the demons which gave the magicians of Egypt power to perform the miracles in the days of Moses and were worshipped as gods in Egypt may also be imprisoned in the pit. "For I will go through the land of Egypt on that night, and will strike down all the firstborn in the land of Egypt, both man and beast; *and against all the gods of Egypt I will execute judgments—I am the LORD*" (Exod. 12:12, emphasis added). This verse seems to indicate that God judged the demon spirits who were masquerading as gods in Egypt. However, it is uncertain whether "executed judgements" against these demon spirits means that they were sent to the pit. Thus, reasonable minds may differ on this issue.

When Jesus Christ dealt with the demons in the man from Gerasenes, the demons requested that Jesus not command them to go to the abyss:

"Then they sailed to the country of the Gerasenes, which is opposite Galilee. And when He had come out onto the land, He was met by a man from the city who was possessed with demons; and who had not put on any clothing for a long time, and was not living in a house, but in the tombs. Seeing Jesus, he cried out and fell before Him, and said in a loud voice, 'What business do we have with each other, Jesus, Son of the Most High God? I beg You, do not torment me.' For He had commanded the unclean spirit to come out of the man… And Jesus asked him, 'What is your name?' And he said, 'Legion'; for many demons had entered him. *They were imploring Him not to command them to go away into the abyss*" (Luke 8:26-31, emphasis added).

Although not stated in Scripture, it is conceivable that in previous encounters with demons, Jesus Christ had sent other demons to the abyss. This might be the reason why the demons thought that Jesus Christ was going to command them to go to the abyss this time also. It is my personal conviction that the Authority of the Believer can also be used to command the demon spirits to go to the abyss/pit and be confined there. This is my practice. I do not want one of them to escape. I ask God to have the holy angels remove them, to destroy them, and to bring them to the pit. There is nothing in Scripture that instructs believers to have mercy or pity on the demons. Rather, we are to exercise mercy and compassion on people.

HOW DEMONS AFFECT THE BELIEVER

HOW DEMONIC BONDAGES DEVELOP

A demonic bondage can develop in several ways including abuse, fear, a traumatic experience, or involvement in the occult. A demonic bondage can also develop when the believer opens the door (either through unrepented sin or deception) and surrenders a room or an area of his life to the powers of darkness. "Neither give place to the devil" (Eph. 4:27 KJV). The Greek word for "place" is *tópos* from which we get the English word topography and can mean an opportunity, region, area, locality, or room.[14] When the believer sins, he gives Satan ground, a place, or a room in his life. A believer who sins and does not repent after being convicted by the Holy Spirit opens a door to the powers of darkness.

The believer will not necessarily develop a demonic bondage in his life merely because he sinned one time. However, it is conceivable that a demonic bondage could result if the believer sins one time. For example, a demonic bondage might occur if the believer is involved in occult activities, such as using a ouija board or visiting a psychic for a reading. Generally, however, a demonic bondage is developed through a pattern of insubordination to God over an extended period of time. The practice of sin weakens the believer's will whereby a demon might be able to exert enough control over the believer to create a bondage. This occurs when the believer willfully exposes himself or herself to worldly influences, gives into temptation, ignores the conviction of the Holy Spirit, and fails to repent of sin. Demonic activity is sometimes revealed by the believer's inability to overcome a particular sin. The Holy Spirit is greater and more powerful than the flesh. If the believer merely has a flesh sin habit, he should be able to break and forsake the habit. Of course, not in his own strength but through prayer, reading the Word of God, and the power of the Holy Spirit. However, the believer must exercise caution to not automatically blame a flesh sin habit on a demon spirit. Some flesh sin habits may take many years to break. But if the believer discovers a sin area in his or her life that cannot be broken over an extended period of time, then consideration should be given that it is not merely a flesh sin habit, but a demonic bondage.

THE BELIEVER CANNOT BE POSSESSED (OWNED) BY A DEMON

If the believer is in bondage to a demon spirit, where does the bondage originate? Is the demon spirit outside of the believer or inside? Of course, a demon can oppress the believer from outside the body, but can the demon who is creating the bondage be operating from inside the believer? A very controversial issue is whether a born-again Christian can be "demon possessed." There are several passages of Scripture that shed light on this issue.

The believer has been bought by Jesus Christ

"You were bought with a price; do not become slaves of men" (1 Cor. 7:23).

The believer belongs to Jesus Christ

"You are not in the flesh but in the Spirit, if indeed the Spirit of God dwells in you. But if anyone does not have the Spirit of Christ, he does not belong to Him" (Rom. 8:9).

The believer is owned by Jesus Christ

"Do you not know that your body is a temple of the Holy Spirit who is in you, whom you have from God, and that you are not your own? For you have been bought with a price: therefore glorify God in your body" (1 Cor. 6:19-20).

The believer is sealed by Jesus Christ

"Do not grieve the Holy Spirit of God, by whom you were sealed for the day of redemption" (Eph. 4:30).

The believer is kept by Jesus Christ

"I give eternal life to them, and they will never perish; and no one will snatch them out of My hand" (John 10:28).

The good news is that if demon possession is defined as

a demon claiming ownership of the believer, then a born-again Christian could never be demon possessed. Scripture is crystal clear on this point.

DEMONS CAN EXERT PARTIAL CONTROL OVER AREAS IN A BELIEVER'S LIFE

Some of the confusion on whether or not a believer can be demon possessed arises because of how a certain Greek word is translated in some versions of the Bible. The Greek word *daimonizomai* is often translated "demon possession" in some versions of the Bible.[15] This is not exactly accurate. Demon possession implies ownership. A more accurate translation of this Greek word would be "demonized," or "under the control of one or more demons."[16]

Although the believer can never be demon possessed, demon spirits can exercise partial control over areas (rooms) in a believer's life. So, the next question that arises is whether demons can exert control from inside the believer, or is it merely outside? In other words, can a demon invade, infect, or trespass the believer? Some will argue that a demon cannot dwell inside a born-again Christian. They base this belief on several premises:

1. Every Christian has the Holy Spirit.
2. The Holy Spirit cannot dwell in the same body with an evil spirit.
3. All demons immediately leave when the Holy Spirit comes to live inside the believer.

Based on these premises, many conclude that a demon spirit cannot dwell in a born-again Christian. We must evaluate each of these premises to determine if the Word of

God supports these premises. If any of these premises are wrong, then the conclusion may be wrong.

Does every Christian have the Holy Spirit?

Premise No. 1 is that every Christian has the Holy Spirit. It is a biblical fact that every Christian has the Holy Spirit: "You are not in the flesh but in the Spirit, if indeed the Spirit of God dwells in you. But if anyone does not have the Spirit of Christ, he does not belong to Him" (Rom. 8:9). Based on this Scripture, we can confidently state that every person who has accepted God's offer of a pardon has the Holy Spirit living within them. However, we all recognize that it is possible for the Holy Spirit to reside in the believer, but not actually control every area in his or her life.

Can demons dwell in the same body with the Holy Spirit?

Premise No. 2 is that the Holy Spirit cannot dwell in the same body with an evil spirit. To the surprise of many, there is nothing in Scripture that explicitly states the Holy Spirit cannot dwell in the same body with an evil spirit. There is nothing. Yet, there is also nothing in Scripture that states the Holy Spirit can dwell in the same body with an evil spirit. You can find verses that state the believer is a new creation in Christ, the believer has been redeemed, and the believer is owned by Jesus Christ, but none of these passages squarely address this very narrow issue. Many Christians want to believe that the Holy Spirit cannot dwell in the same body with an evil spirit, because to believe otherwise, makes them feel vulnerable.

We do know that the Holy Spirit can dwell in a body where the presence of evil exists. Believers will say that

Jesus Christ lives in their heart. Yet, some believer's hearts are often filled with great evil. "Out of the heart come evil thoughts, murders, adulteries, fornications, thefts, false witness, slanders" (Matt. 15:19). Let me ask you a few personal questions:

> As a believer, have you ever thought about committing adultery or entertained a sexual fantasy?
>
> As a believer, have you ever stolen anything?
>
> As a believer, have you ever thought about killing another person?
>
> As a believer, have you ever been greedy?
>
> As a believer, have you ever been angry or bitter over an extended period?

Think of what the Holy Spirit has to contend with in many carnal believers' lives. The Holy Spirit dwells in many believers where there is unrepented sin such as murder, adultery, rebellion, lust, hate, bitterness, greed, and violence. Does the Holy Spirit leave the believer every time he sins and fails to repent? Is the Holy Spirit's presence in the believer similar to a revolving door? Of course not! Thus, the Holy Spirit can dwell in a body where the presence of evil exists.

Do all demons leave when a person is saved?

Premise No. 3 is that all demons immediately leave when the Holy Spirit comes to live in a person. The logical conclusion of this premise is that even if a person has been involved in witchcraft or Satanism, was a mass murderer, or had a thirty-year pornography or cocaine addiction, in every instance and without exception, all demons immediately leave when the person accepts Jesus Christ as his or her Lord and Savior. I do not believe this is true in every case. A person prior to receiving Jesus Christ as Lord and Savior was part of the Kingdom of Satan:

> "You were dead in your trespasses and sins, in which you formerly walked according to the course of this world, according to the prince of the power of the air, of the spirit that is now working in the sons of disobedience. Among them we too all formerly lived in the lusts of our flesh, indulging the desires of the flesh and of the mind, and were by nature children of wrath, even as the rest" (Eph. 2:1-3).

This passage indicates that the "prince of the power of the air" commonly known as Satan is working in the sons of disobedience. Unbelievers are the sons of disobedience. Thus, it is apparent that demon spirits can enter unbelievers to cause them to indulge the desires of the flesh. However, this does not mean that all unbelievers have demon spirits dwelling in them. But it does mean that some unbelievers may have demons dwelling in them.

When a person receives Jesus Christ as Lord and Savior, the Holy Spirit enters him or her. As the power and presence of the Holy Spirit comes in a person, many of the demons leave immediately. However, there is no guarantee that all of the demons leave. It is possible that some demons remain in the believer. In the Old Testament, God gave the Promised Land to the Children of Israel. The inhabitants of the land did not immediately move out. The Children of Israel had to battle the inhabitants of the land and force them to leave. There is nothing in Scripture that explicitly states all demonic bondages are broken immediately and all demon spirits leave when a person receives Jesus Christ. The reality is that there can be demon spirits remaining in the believer who entered prior to salvation.

Most believers do not understand the difference between a flesh sin habit and a demon spirit trying to exert control over them. Some will assume a sin bondage is only a flesh sin habit. Others who discern they are in the midst of a spiritual battle will automatically assume that the attack is from without and not from within them. Keep in mind, it is often the hidden and disguised nature of demonic activity that gives believers a false sense of security that they are not subject to demonic oppression or indwelling. Naturally, the spiritual problem could simply be that the believer needs to crucify his flesh, yield every area in his life to the Holy Spirit, develop a consistent prayer life, study the Word of God, and have healthy Christian fellowship. However, in some cases, the attack could quite possibly originate from within the person. In conclusion, fault-finding, violence, gossip, frustration, hate, lust, suicide thoughts, gluttony, and other sins can be merely works of the flesh and can be brought on by many reasons, including psychological or physical challenges. They can also be areas controlled by demons from within the believer. This is not just my opinion but the opinion of several biblical scholars. One such biblical scholar is Fred Dickason who was on the faculty of the Moody Bible Institute for thirty-five years. He was a professor and chairman of the Theology Department. He wrote a book entitled "Demon Possession & the Christian."[17] He arrived at the same conclusion after counselling numerous Christians who had demon spirits within them.

TEST TO DETERMINE DEMON
SPIRIT'S PRESENCE

There are many Christians leaders who sit on the sidelines and debate whether a demon spirit can cause a spiritual bondage from within the believer. This is like three people staring at a bush and arguing whether there is a rabbit inside the bush. Imagine the first person has a PhD in rabbit psychology and teaches at a university. He is so knowledgeable about rabbits that his students and colleagues refer to him as Dr. Rabbit. He pulls out a scholarly treatise on rabbits which states that rabbits never hide in these types of bushes. Imagine the second person is the president of a commercial rabbit business which has two thousand employees. He has been raising rabbits for more than thirty years. He often gets invited to speak at state and national rabbit conferences. He argues that he has never personally seen a rabbit hiding in this type of bush in his entire professional life. Imagine the third person is a small family farmer. He never went to college. He does not have a PhD and is not a president of a large business. However, he has a lot of common sense. He suggests that instead of speculating or guessing whether a rabbit is in the bush, they merely "kick the bush" and see if a rabbit jumps out. The other two frankly admit that they have never even thought of this option.

When the disciples told Jesus that "even the demons are subject to us in your name," His response was very interesting:

> "Nevertheless, do not rejoice in this, that the spirits are subject to you, but rejoice that your names are recorded in heaven. At that very time He rejoiced greatly in the Holy Spirit, and said,

'I praise You, O Father, Lord of heaven and earth, that *You have hidden these things from the wise and intelligent and have revealed them to infants.* Yes, Father, for this way was well-pleasing in Your sight'" (Luke 10:20-21, emphasis added).

Jesus Christ seemed to imply that the reality of the spiritual world and the believer's authority over the demon spirits is often hidden from the wise and the intelligent – the intellectuals of this world. Even many Christian leaders who say they believe the Bible, often do not believe in the reality of demon spirits and the possibility that they can influence or attack the believer.

There is a simple test to "kick the bush." You begin praying with the person, taking your authority "in Christ" and commanding that if there are any demon spirits within the person that they manifest (or reveal) their presence. Bringing the Authority of the Believer directly against the demon spirits will get their attention. You could pray as follows:

"Heavenly Father, I take my spiritual authority which I have as I am 'seated in Christ' at your right hand, and I bind the demon spirits that may be present in [Name of Person] and I command them to manifest and reveal their presence."

DEMONIC MANIFESTATIONS

If there are demon spirits present in the person, they may manifest their presence. There are both subjective and objective manifestations. A subjective manifestation is where the person feels a definite sensation within them when you bring the Authority of the Believer against the demon spirits. Subjective manifestations may include, but are not limited to, a sharp pain, a sudden fear (like they want to just get up and leave as quick as they can), hearing voices in their head, extreme wicked thoughts, their heart begins to race, a slight tightening sensation in the throat, or a tingling sensation in the body. These are all subjective manifestations. However, a subjective manifestation must be kept in the proper perspective because it may relate to a psychological or emotional issue, and not a demonic presence.

There is also an objective manifestation. An objective manifestation is where demon spirits take over the vocal cords of the person in response to bringing the Authority of the Believer against them. As described in the Bible, there are instances in which a demon spirit dwelling in a person had the ability to take over the vocal cords and speak through the person. When a demon speaks through a person, it is objective evidence that a demon spirit is within the person. There is no longer any need to speculate. Keep in mind, there is also the possibility a person may have a demonic stronghold and there will be no subjective or objective demonic manifestation. In testing whether a demon spirit is present, you might have a false negative, but you will never have a false positive.

BREAKING DEMONIC BONDAGES

It is often very difficult to determine if a demonic bondage originates inside or outside of the believer. As a practical matter, it is almost irrelevant whether the demon spirit is operating from inside or outside the believer. The demonic bondage can be broken even if there is uncertainty whether the demon spirit is operating inside or outside. The method of breaking a spiritual bondage does not depend on whether the demon spirit is inside or outside a person.

Spiritual bondages are broken by the believer shutting the doors to the powers of darkness, bringing the Authority of the Believer against the demon spirits, and commanding them to leave and go to the pit. A more comprehensive analysis on the removal of demon spirits is addressed in Chapter 13. Always remember, the presence of a demon spirit is a secondary issue. The primary issue is to make sure that all doors are closed, that you have repented of all sin, that you have asked God to reveal any deception in your life, and that all areas (rooms) in your life have been surrendered to the Holy Spirit.

ACTIVITIES OF DEMONS

SCOPE OF SATAN'S ACTIVITIES

The Lord Jesus Christ recognized the activities of demon spirits. Yet, in our modern world, many people do not believe that demon spirits are constantly trying to obtain control of their lives. Satan has blinded many people from the reality of his activity on the earth. Sadly, this spiritual blindness also applies to many believers and churches. Nevertheless, Satan has a broad scope of activity. We are going to do a quick survey of some of the activities that are set forth in the Word of God.

Stealing the Word

> "When anyone hears the word of the kingdom and does not understand it, the evil one comes and snatches away what has been sown in his heart. This is the one on whom seed was sown beside the road" (Matt. 13:19).

This passage reveals that after the Word of God is proclaimed, Satan will attempt to steal it from a lost person's heart to hinder or prevent the person from getting saved. We need to combat this with prayer. This means that either before or after you share the Gospel with a person, you need to pray that Satan would not be able to steal the Word of God that is planted in the person's heart.

Blinding minds

> "Even if our gospel is veiled, it is veiled to those who are perishing, in whose case the god of this world has blinded the minds of the unbelieving so that they might not see the light of the gospel of the glory of Christ, who is the image of God" (2 Cor. 4:3-4).

This passage reveals that Satan is able to blind a person's mind from seeing his or her need for a savior. This is also combated by prayer. You can also take your spiritual authority which you have as you are "seated in Christ" and bind the demon spirits who are blinding and hindering a person from understanding the Gospel and seeing their need to receive Jesus Christ as Lord and Savior.

False religions

> "I am afraid that, as the serpent deceived Eve by his craftiness, your minds will be led astray from the simplicity and purity *of devotion* to Christ. For if one comes and preaches another Jesus whom we have not preached, or you receive a different spirit which you have not received, or a different gospel which you have not accepted, you bear *this* beautifully" (2 Cor. 11:3-4).

Satan is behind every false religion. A false religion may

refer to Jesus Christ, but it is often not the Jesus described in the Bible. The Jesus described in the Bible is the Son of God, who gave his life as a sacrifice for sin, rose from the dead, and is the only way to God. He is a different Jesus than what many of these false religions proclaim.

False doctrine

> "The Spirit explicitly says that in later times some will fall away from the faith, paying attention to deceitful spirits and doctrines of demons" (1 Tim. 4:1).

False doctrine often arises in a church because individual Christians and leaders do not take the time to study the Word of God. Also, many read the Word of God with preconceived ideas. It is not sufficient for you to merely rely on me, a pastor, or some other Christian leader to understand the Bible. Learning from knowledgeable Bible teachers is important. Yet, you must also study the Bible for yourself and ask the Holy Spirit to open your mind to the truth of the Word of God.

Planting doubt

> "Now the serpent was more crafty than any beast of the field which the LORD God had made… The woman said to the serpent, 'From the fruit of the trees of the garden we may eat; but from the fruit of the tree which is in the middle of the garden, God has said, You shall not eat from it or touch it, or you will die.' The serpent said to the woman, 'You surely will not die! For God knows that in the day you eat from it your eyes will be

opened, and you will be like God, knowing good
and evil'" (Gen. 3:1-5).

Satan tempted Eve to doubt what God had commanded.
Satan will also tempt believers to doubt God, including
His promises, goodness, faithfulness, sovereignty, existence,
Word, power, love, and warnings against sin. We need to
reject these doubts.

Accusing

> "Now the salvation, and the power, and the king-
> dom of our God and the authority of His Christ
> have come, for the accuser [Satan] of our breth-
> ren has been thrown down, he who accuses them
> before our God day and night" (Rev. 12:10).

Satan is the father of guilt and condemnation. He wants
you to feel ashamed. Satan wants you to feel like you need
to pay for your sins. When you sin, the Holy Spirit will
convict you, but He never condemns you. The Holy Spirit
convicts you primarily for two reasons. First, to restore
your fellowship with God so the goodness of God can continue to flow into your life. Second, the Holy Spirit convicts you to prevent an open door which might allow the
powers of darkness to create a spiritual bondage in your life.

Lying and deception

> "You are of *your* father the devil, and you want to
> do the desires of your father. He was a murderer
> from the beginning, and does not stand in the
> truth because there is no truth in him. Whenever
> he speaks a lie, he speaks from his own *nature*,
> for he is a liar and the father of lies" (John 8:44).

Satan is a liar. As we discussed in Chapter 5, one of the three ways that Satan can have access to your life is through deception. The Belt of Truth of the Armor of God will protect you from four categories of lies. There are other lies, but there are four primary categories including lies about yourself, lies about others, lies about God, and lies about Satan. You must ask God to reveal the lies you have believed.

Sexual temptations

> "Stop depriving one another, except by agreement for a time, so that you may devote yourselves to prayer, and come together again so that Satan will not tempt you because of your lack of self-control" (1 Cor. 7:5).

Satan tempts people with sexual sins prior to marriage. He also wants to destroy a couple's sexual relationship after they are married. If you had sex before marriage, or after marriage with a person other than your spouse, you need to repent of that sin and shut the door. Many do not realize that Satan tries to destroy a couple's sex life after marriage by using doors that were opened prior to marriage. Even if you had sex with a person whom you later married (and you were a believer at that time), you still need to repent of that sin and shut the door. It does not matter that you committed that sin twenty years ago. If you have not repented of that sin, you are still giving a place (or room) for Satan to destroy your relationship with your spouse. Just marrying the person whom you had sex with does not close the door if you were a believer when you sinned.

There are four areas you must avoid to prevent Satan from obtaining a foothold in your sex life:

1. Do not have sex with someone other than your spouse.

2. Do not allow immoral thoughts to linger in your mind (*i.e.*, fantasizing about having sex with a person that you are not married to).

3. Do not give up emotionally on your spouse.

4. Do not have romantic daydreams about someone other than your spouse. This includes having an emotional affair with a person and justifying it in your mind by claiming they are just a friend.

Jealousy and selfish ambition

"If you have bitter jealousy and selfish ambition in your heart, do not be arrogant and *so* lie against the truth. This wisdom is not that which comes down from above, but is earthly, natural, demonic" (Jam. 3:14-15).

Believers must constantly guard their hearts against jealousy and selfish ambition. We must watch our motives. We must do the right thing with the right motives, or we will lose our reward.

Trials and tribulations

"Do not fear what you are about to suffer. Behold, the devil is about to cast some of you into prison, so that you will be tested, and you will have tribulation for ten days. Be faithful until death, and I will give you the crown of life" (Rev. 2:10).

Remember what was discussed in Chapter 8. Satan

gains power over the believer not necessarily through persecution but giving into the fear of persecution.

Hindering ministry

> "We, brethren, having been taken away from you for a short while—in person, not in spirit—were all the more eager with great desire to see your face. For we wanted to come to you—I, Paul, more than once—and *yet* Satan hindered us" (1 Thess. 2:17-18).

Satan can hinder a ministry. Thus, believers need to constantly pray for churches and ministries because they are all under attack by the powers of darkness. If you are a member of a church, you need to pray for your church and pastor.

False disciples

> "Such men are false apostles, deceitful workers, disguising themselves as apostles of Christ. No wonder, for even Satan disguises himself as an angel of light. Therefore it is not surprising if his servants also disguise themselves as servants of righteousness, whose end will be according to their deeds" (2 Cor. 11:13-15).

What is a false disciple? It could mean many things. What comes to my mind is people who attend church and claim they are a Christian but have never actually fulfilled the eligibility requirements to receive God's offer of a pardon. They may admit they have sinned. They may intellectually believe the Gospel, but they have never truly repented of their sin and surrendered their life to Jesus

Christ. These people are false disciples because they have a false salvation.

Devouring people

> "Be of sober *spirit*, be on the alert. Your adversary, the devil, prowls around like a roaring lion, seeking someone to devour" (1 Pet. 5:8).

Satan is a roaring lion seeking someone to devour. Do not be a victim of a self-inflicted wound because you gave a weapon to Satan to use against you, to devour you, by opening a door. Remember, there are three ways you can open a door and give a weapon to the powers of darkness. First, failing to repent of sin you have committed after salvation even though the Holy Spirit convicted you about the sin. Second, deception in your life. And third, giving in to the fear of persecution. You also need to pray every day, study the Word of God, and have good Christian fellowship. My friend and I were trying to repair a plow. We needed to take off a bolt. I could not get the bolt off by myself. My friend could not get the bolt off by himself either; however, he had two large wrenches. My friend used one of the wrenches and I used the other one. Together we got the bolt off. There are times in life when we need other people. God designed it this way. There are certain problems where we must rely on others for help. This is the purpose of having good friends. Having good Christian fellowship minimizes the chances that you will be devoured by the enemy.

Supernatural strength

> "He [Jesus] had commanded the unclean spirit to come out of the man. For it had seized him

many times; and he was bound with chains and shackles and kept under guard, and *yet* he would break his bonds and be driven by the demon into the desert" (Luke 8:29).

People under demonic power can exhibit extreme or supernatural strength. This is often seen in the occult and certain practices in some martial arts.

Occult practices

> "There shall not be found among you anyone who makes his son or his daughter pass through the fire, one who uses divination, one who practices witchcraft, or one who interprets omens, or a sorcerer, or one who casts a spell, or a medium, or a spiritist, or one who calls up the dead" (Deut. 18:10-11).

Occult practices include, but are not limited to, reading horoscopes, using tarot cards, visiting a psychic, watching occult movies, playing with a ouija board, and participating in a séance—even if just for fun. If you have dabbled in any of these occult activities after you were saved, you need to repent of the sin and shut the door.

There are other activities of demon spirits that perhaps need to be analysed more closely because of the controversy surrounding them.

PHYSICAL ILLNESS

Before I discuss the topic of physical illness, I want to explain my approach in interpreting the Word of God. I believe in the Verbal Plenary Inspiration view of the Word of God. This view is held by many evangelical churches. This view holds that every single word and every part of the Bible is inspired by God.[18] However, God did not bypass the personality of the writer or his writing style. Yet, at the same time, the Holy Spirit was able to ensure that the final product was exactly what God intended. So, I believe the Bible is accurate, true, and can be fully trusted regardless of whether I fully understand it. Having laid that foundation, I believe that demon spirits can be the root cause of some, but not all, physical illnesses.

Physical illnesses can be caused by a demon spirit

> "There was a woman who for eighteen years *had a sickness caused by a spirit*; and she was bent double, and could not straighten up at all" (Luke 13:11, emphasis added).

It is clear from this passage that the woman's physical infirmity was caused by a demon spirit. We do not know for sure, but quite possibly there was no physical reason why the woman was bent over. Thus, merely treating her medically may not have healed her because it was the demon spirit's presence that caused the woman to be bent over. Interestingly, there is no reason to believe from the passage that others around her thought she was afflicted by a demon spirit. In other words, she showed no obvious signs of demonic oppression or indwelling. An illness caused by a demon can have all the symptoms of a physical illness, but a medical examination may fail to find the physical cause of the illness.

Failure to diagnose a physical illness does not mean it is demonic

An illness should not automatically be attributed to a demon spirit merely because there is no apparent cause of the illness. Medicine is not sufficiently advanced to diagnose and treat every illness. Also, an illness with an unknown physical cause can be psychosomatic. Such an illness often appears when there are mental or emotional difficulties in a person's life. An illness that is psychosomatic may not be directly and solely related to demon spirits.

Physical illness can be the result of sin

There is a false doctrine held by some Christians who contend *all* sickness is caused by unrepented sin. In response to this false doctrine, some Christians have gone to the other extreme and assert that physical illness is never God's discipline for unrepented sin. Many think it is cruel to even suggest that a person might be sick because of some unrepented sin in their life. Yet, the Bible clearly states that an illness can be caused by sin:

> "A man was there who had been ill for thirty-eight years... Jesus said to him, 'Get up, pick up your pallet and walk.' Immediately the man became well, and picked up his pallet and *began* to walk... Afterward Jesus found him in the temple and said to him, '*Behold, you have become well; do not sin anymore, so that nothing worse happens to you*'" (John 5:5-9 & 14, emphasis added).

This passage appears to suggest that the man's illness was a result of sin, because Jesus said, "do not sin any more so that nothing worse happens to you." The Apostle Paul also stated that some believers in the church at Corinth were sick because they had unrepented sin in their life:

> "A man must examine himself, and in so doing he is to eat of the bread and drink of the cup. For he who eats and drinks, eats and drinks judgment to himself if he does not judge the body rightly. *For this reason many among you are weak and sick, and a number sleep.* But if we judged ourselves rightly, we would not be judged. But when we are judged, we are disciplined by the Lord so that we will not be condemned along with the world" (1 Cor. 11:28-32, emphasis added).

The believer must be sensitive to the Holy Spirit because a sickness can be God's discipline when there is unrepented sin in a Christian's life but not always.

Physical illness can be unrelated to demon spirits

A person can have an illness that has a physical cause that is completely unrelated to demon spirits. An example of this situation is recorded in Matthew:

> "As Jesus went on from there, two blind men followed Him, crying out, 'Have mercy on us, Son of David!' When He entered the house, the blind men came up to Him, and Jesus said to them, 'Do you believe that I am able to do this?' They said to Him, 'Yes, Lord.' Then He touched their eyes, saying, 'It shall be done to you according to your faith.' And their eyes were opened" (Matt. 9:27-30).

It is apparent that Jesus cured the men of a physical abnormality. He did not seek to cast out demon spirits. The blindness had a completely physical cause. Also, there is no indication that the blindness had anything to do with unrepented sin in their lives. Not every illness is the result of sin or demon spirits in a person's life. Thus, the believer must ask God for discernment in trying to determine whether an illness has a physical or spiritual origin.

MENTAL ILLNESS

Demon spirits can cause mental illness including behavioral disorders. Demon spirits can possess people and cause them to act irrationally and dangerous. They can also cause obsessive behavior, depression, anxiety, multiple personalities, stress, and paranoia. It is my conviction that some, but not all, mental illness in our society is demonic in origin. An example of a demon spirit which caused a mental illness is described in the Gospel of Mark:

> "They came to the other side of the sea, into the country of the Gerasenes. When He got out of the boat, immediately a man from the tombs with an unclean spirit met Him, and he had his dwelling among the tombs. And no one was able to bind him anymore, even with a chain; because he had often been bound with shackles and chains, and the chains had been torn apart by him, and the shackles broken into pieces, and no one was strong enough to subdue him. Constantly night and day, he was screaming among the tombs and in the mountains, and gashing himself with stones" (Mark 5:1-5).

This passage contains a description of an extreme example of a man afflicted by demon spirits. He probably would have been institutionalized if he had lived in our modern age. He had his dwelling among the tombs. He had often been bound with shackles and chains. However, he would tear apart the chains and break the shackles with his incredible strength. He must have been in severe mental anguish because he cried night and day. He was also a danger to himself because he would gash himself with stones. He was cutting himself. However, after Jesus evicted the demon spirits, the man was healed completely. "*The people* came to see what it was that had happened. They came to Jesus and observed the man who had been demon possessed sitting down, *clothed and in his right mind*, the very man who had had the 'legion'; and they became frightened" (Mark 5:15, emphasis added). Most people who are oppressed or indwelt by demon spirits will never experience anything comparable to what this man experienced.

Mental illness is not always caused by demon spirits

Mental illness is not always directly and solely caused by demon spirits. The human mind can be affected, not only by demon spirits, but also by an individual's genetics, physical challenges, past trauma, abuse, family background, environment, and other factors. It is possible that demon spirits may be present exploiting weaknesses and traumas from childhood or other circumstances. Thus, demons can be a contributing factor to a mental illness, but they may not be the sole factor in every case. It is also possible that a chemical imbalance in the human body, unrelated to demon spirits, can affect a person's behavior and may require medical intervention. Where the demons are merely a contributing factor to a mental illness, but not the sole factor, there can be physical, mental, and emotional wounds that often remain even after the demons have departed. These wounds must also be treated.

Christian psychologists often do not recognize demonic influence

I appreciate those who have dedicated their lives to study human behavior and how the mind is affected by a person's environment, background, family history, medical condition, and other factors. However, too often those who study in this area do not believe in the supernatural realms. Even some Christian psychologists are blinded to the reality of Satan's power. Many Christian psychologists have never even had one formal class on spiritual warfare or how demon spirits can affect the human mind, even if they attended a Christian school. Many perhaps believe in theory that demon spirits can afflict people because to state otherwise would be to deny the Word of God. In practice, however, many do not believe a demon can afflict a person and never investigate that possibility when counseling a person.

A Christian psychologist's approach to counseling is often significantly influenced and shaped by his or her worldview. The worldview of many Christian psychologists often does not take into account the existence of demon spirits. For example, if a person states that they are hearing voices in their head, I suspect that many psychologists never seriously consider that the person is actually hearing voices. They never seriously consider that the person is oppressed or indwelt by a demon spirit. Of course, the person may have a mental illness that is completely unrelated to demon spirits. Maybe the person just needs in-depth counseling and medication. My goal is not to have Christian psychologists throw out everything they have learned at a secular university or their methodologies. Instead, what I suggest is they merely consider putting an additional tool in their toolbox. To dig a little deeper and give consideration that some mental illnesses may have a spiritual origin.

SATAN AND MUSIC

It is quite conceivable that before Satan's fall, he was a musician before the throne of God. Satan is quite possibly the greatest musician since the dawn of time:

> "Thou hast been in Eden the garden of God; every precious stone was thy covering, the sardius, topaz, and the diamond, the beryl, the onyx, and the jasper, the sapphire, the emerald, and the carbuncle, and gold: *the workmanship of thy tabrets and of thy pipes was prepared in thee in the day that thou wast created*" (Ezek. 28:13 KJV, emphasis added).

The Bible in reference to Satan states, "the workmanship of thy tabrets and of thy pipes was prepared in thee in the day that thou wast created." Tabrets comes from the Hebrew word *toph* which means a timbrel or tambourine.[19] Thus, Satan might be different from any other being known to man. Did God create musical instruments in Satan before his fall? Can Satan generate and create music internally? Was Satan the first musician? The Bible does not clearly answer these questions, but this passage gives us something to ponder.

Spiritual influence of music

Music has a powerful spiritual influence that can be used to further the Kingdom of God and the Kingdom of Satan. Music under the presence of the Holy Spirit can cause demon spirits to flee. Thus, it is no wonder why the demon spirit left King Saul when David played music to God. If you recall the story, an evil spirit was afflicting Saul. David was asked to play his harp for Saul. "It came about whenever the evil spirit from God came to Saul, David would take the harp and play it with his hand; and Saul would be refreshed and be well, and the evil spirit would depart from him" (1 Sam. 16:23). Evidently, the evil spirit left when David played music anointed by the Holy Spirit.

Factors when evaluating music to enjoy

Music can be used to further the Kingdom of Satan. Demon spirits can inspire men to write music. Thus, certain songs can be spiritually evil and be a stumbling block. You should evaluate various factors when deciding if it is proper to listen to a particular song or type of music. These factors include:

1. Are the lyrics of the song contrary to the Word of God?

2. Are you convicted by the Holy Spirit, or does your conscience bother you during, or after listening to the song or type of music?

3. Does the song or type of music provoke vain imaginations, violence, or worldliness? Vain imagination is where you enter a fantasy world where you are a rock star or a famous Christian musician, singing on stage to thousands for your own glory. Of

course, you may justify it because you are singing for Jesus, but if you examine your daydreams carefully, you might notice how you get part of the glory or fame.

COMMUNICATION WITH THE DECEASED

Many wonder if a person can contact the spirit of someone who has died. Perhaps you have heard stories about someone who contacted a deceased person who was able to provide detailed information that only they would have known. A medium is a person who claims they can contact the spirits of the dead. Often, the medium allows a spirit to enter them and speak through them to the people gathered for a séance. The term "familiar spirit" is used in the King James version of the Bible that some interpret as a demon spirit that is familiar with a deceased person.

Prohibition against contacting the deceased

The Bible has an absolute prohibition against attempting to contact those who are deceased and familiar spirits. "Regard not them that have familiar spirits, neither seek after wizards, to be defiled by them: I am the Lord your God." (Lev. 19:31 KJV). God established this prohibition for several reasons. First, the real person who has died is in either Heaven or Hell and no human can successfully initiate contact with them. Second, any contact that is made will only be made with a demon spirit who will counterfeit and pose as the spirit of the deceased person.

Demon spirits can impersonate the deceased

Individuals who participate in séances often believe they have actually contacted a deceased person. Participants will ask very intimate questions of the spirit which no one could possibly know except the deceased person. When the spirit answers correctly, the participants believe this must be the deceased person. However, demon spirits have the ability to impersonate a deceased person. A familiar spirit, that is a demon spirit, may have previously watched or obtained information about the deceased person. Thus, the demon spirit may have the knowledge to answer the questions correctly and deceive the participants in the séance.

There is a story in the Bible where King Saul attempted to contact Samuel who had previously died:

> "Then Saul said to his servants, 'Seek for me a woman who is a medium, that I may go to her and inquire of her.' And his servants said to him, *'Behold, there is a woman who is a medium at Endor.'* Then Saul disguised himself by putting on other clothes, and went, he and two men with him, and they came to the woman by night; and he said, 'Conjure up for me, please, and bring up for me whom I shall name to you.'… Then the woman said, 'Whom shall I bring up for you?' And he said, 'Bring up Samuel for me.' *When the woman saw Samuel, she cried out with a loud voice; and the woman spoke to Saul, saying, 'Why have you deceived me? For you are Saul'"* (1 Sam. 28:7-12, emphasis added).

The witch of En-dor was a spiritualist and was under demonic power. When she tried to contact deceased people, she probably believed she contacted the actual deceased person. However, in reality she only contacted a familiar spirit posing as the deceased person. It is debatable among biblical scholars, but it at least appears that the witch of En-dor did *not* contact a demon spirit during this encounter. Unknown to her, God the Father, by his divine sovereignty and authority, permitted her to contact the real Samuel. In fact, she was shocked when the real Samuel came up. "When the woman saw Samuel, she cried out with a loud voice; and the woman spoke to Saul, saying, 'Why have you deceived me?'" (1 Sam. 28:12). When the real Samuel came up, she may have been shocked and surprised because she was used to contacting only familiar spirits. It must be understood, it was not the power of the medium which brought up the real Samuel. A medium has no power to contact the actual spirit of a deceased person. A medium can only contact a demon spirit posing as a deceased person. Of course, in many cases, there are no demon spirits present, and the participants are deceived by a "fake medium" who uses human trickery. This is likely the explanation for some encounters that people experience during a séance.

Demon spirits inhabiting homes

Some people claim to have experienced supernatural encounters which cause them to believe a house is haunted. A lady once told me that after her husband died, a lightbulb in her house flickered on and off. She was convinced that her deceased husband was trying to contact her. Others claim to have seen an image of a spirit, heard voices, or observed unusual manifestations in their home. Of course, this may merely be a person's vivid imagination. As I previously stated, when a person dies, his or her soul immediately goes to Heaven or Hell. A person's soul or spirit does not remain on the earth after death. Yet, it could also be, in some cases, that the people living in the home are not imagining some of this activity. It is quite possible there could be spirits present in the home. They are not the spirits of those who have previously died but are demon spirits. They may be in the home preying on the fears and anxieties of the people living there.

This kind of intrusion can be immediately stopped by bringing the Authority of the Believer against the demon spirits and commanding them to leave and go to the pit. Frankly, once you understand the Authority of the Believer and are willing to pull the trigger against the powers of darkness, you will probably never experience any supernatural manifestation in a home. It may prove just too risky for some of the demons.

SUPERNATURAL MANIFESTATIONS

The Holy Spirit can produce signs and wonders. When God works through the agency of a man or woman to perform a supernatural wonder, as a general rule, the person must have the Holy Spirit. Only those who have repented of their sin, believed the Gospel, trusted in the shed blood of Jesus Christ to pay the penalty for their sin, and have personally received Jesus Christ as Lord and Savior have the Holy Spirit in them.

Demon spirits can counterfeit some signs and wonders

Satan and the demon spirits can perform signs and wonders. "That is, the one whose coming is in accord with the activity of Satan, with all power and signs and false wonders" (2 Thess. 2:9). An example of Satan's ability to perform a miracle was when God transformed Aaron's staff into a serpent and Satan was able to duplicate it:

> "Aaron threw his staff down before Pharaoh and his servants, and it became a serpent. Then Pharaoh also called for the wise men and the sorcerers, and they also, the magicians of Egypt, did the same with their secret arts. For each one threw down his staff and they turned into serpents. But Aaron's staff swallowed up their staffs" (Exod. 7:10-12).

Here, the wise men, the sorcerers, and the magicians of Egypt, were able to duplicate or counterfeit this miracle. They did not use human trickery but supernatural demonic power.

Important principles to prevent deception

Any person that performs a supernatural manifestation and does not have the Holy Spirit is most likely utilizing a demon spirit for the source of power, whether he or she knows it or not. There is no natural energy force that can be tapped to perform supernatural phenomenon apart from a spiritual being. Demon spirits must give humans the energy to perform these feats. Humans do not have any inherent supernatural abilities, latent power in their mind, or electrical energy to perform supernatural manifestations. Furthermore, it is possible for a person to perform a supernatural manifestation and not even be aware that demon spirits are giving him or her this ability.

Some in the martial arts believe that there is a life energy force, sometimes called Ki, that can be developed through meditation. They do not believe the power comes from demon spirits but is merely an energy force based on scientific principles. Once developed, this energy force allegedly can be used to move objects with your mind or perform other supernatural feats. Before I recommitted my life to Jesus Christ, I spent several years training in the martial arts with people who tried to develop and use Ki. The original movie *Star Wars* had a fairly good description of Ki and was called the "force" in that movie. When the movie came out, my martial arts instructors, who were involved in the occult, commented that the people who made the movie must have known about Ki.

Sincere people can still be deceived by Satan

A person can be using demonic power to perform supernatural manifestations even if he claims to have never sought these abilities or tried to develop them. Also, a Christian can have a supernatural counterfeit gift of the Holy Spirit because of an open door, often due to deception, pride or jealousy. A person, even a born-again Christian, can be using demonic power to perform a supernatural manifestation even if his motives are sincere in wanting to heal or help people. My martial arts instructors were very good and kind people. They honestly wanted to help people. Many cannot understand how the supernatural power they possess is demonic when it is being used for good purposes. For instance, some distinguish between "white" and "black" witchcraft. Thus, many believe that how the supernatural power is used will determine whether it is of Satan or God. The error in this belief is that it fails to take into account that there are two separate sources of supernatural power in the world.

The Holy Spirit and Satan can produce supernatural power. The Holy Spirit's power can be used only for good purposes to bring glory and honor to the Lord Jesus Christ. Satan can produce supernatural power that can be used for evil purposes and seemingly good purposes. One may ask, why would Satan use his supernatural power for seemingly good purposes, since he is a very evil spiritual being? It must be recognized that Satan's prime objective is to keep people in the world spiritually blinded, so they do not receive Jesus Christ as Lord and Savior. Satan is willing to use his power to perform works which have seemingly good purposes if it takes the focus off a person's need for a savior from sin or results in deception. Satan knows that the majority of people will automatically believe that a supernatural wonder is from God if it has an apparent good purpose. Consequently, Satan is willing to perform supernatural manifestations, which appear to have good purposes, to further his objective.

SINS OF PAST GENERATIONS

THE BIBLE DOES NOT EXPLAIN EVERYTHING

What is revealed in the Word of God about the spiritual realms is like the tip of an iceberg. God has only explained a very small portion of what is transpiring in the spiritual realms. This is why God requires us to trust him and walk by faith. The Word of God often states a fact on a particular issue but does not always provide a detailed or logical explanation on why or how that fact is true. For example, the Bible clearly states that the Holy Spirit resides in every believer (Rom. 8:9). Each believer has the complete Holy Spirit within them, not just part of the Holy Spirit. Yet, the Bible does not explain how 100 percent of the Holy Spirit can be in me, 100 percent of the Holy Spirit can be in you, and 100 percent of the Holy Spirit can also be in millions of people at the same time. We accept this fact by faith, even though it seems illogical, and we do not fully understand it.

The Bible also does not provide a detailed and logical explanation of the Trinity. The Bible states unequivocally that Jesus Christ is God (Col. 2:9). I want to emphasize that the Bible does not state that Jesus is part of God or merely had godlike qualities. Instead, the Bible clearly states that Jesus is God. The Bible also states the Holy Spirit is God (Acts 5:3-4) and the Father is God (Eph. 4:6). If this is true, based on human logic, there must be three Gods. Yet, the Bible also states that there is only one God (Deut. 6:4). True Christians acknowledge the truth of Scripture regarding the three persons of the Trinity, while at the same time still believe there is only one God. Christians accept these facts by faith, even though many do not fully understand it and sometimes find it difficult to explain to others.

The Bible is a book of absolute and perfect knowledge, but is not a book of total comprehensive knowledge. It does not explain everything. The Bible does not provide a comprehensive and logical explanation for every mystery and apparent contradiction in the Word of God. God wants us to trust Him and believe Him, even when we do not understand and cannot logically explain everything. This is especially true on the topic of demon spirits afflicting little children.

We are going to review two passages of Scripture where a demon spirit was able to afflict a child. The first passage is in Chapter 7 of the Gospel of Mark. "After hearing of Him, *a woman whose little daughter had an unclean spirit*, immediately came and fell at his feet. Now the woman was a Gentile, of the Syrophoencian race. And she kept asking Him to cast the demon out of her daughter" (Mark 7:25-26, emphasis added). Imagine this, the woman's "little daughter" had a demon. The little girl was probably too young to be involved in habitual sin or to open other doors in her life to the powers of darkness. Thus, how did the demon enter her? Scripture does not provide an answer to this question.

Another example of a child being afflicted by a demon spirit is described in Chapter 9 of the Gospel of Mark:

> "One of the crowd answered Him, Teacher, I brought You my son, possessed with a spirit which makes him mute; and whenever it seizes him, it slams him to the ground and he foams at the mouth, and grinds his teeth, and stiffens out.'… When he saw Him [Jesus], immediately the spirit threw him into a convulsion, and falling to the ground, he began rolling around and foaming at the mouth. And He asked his father, *'How long has this been happening to him?' And he said, 'From childhood'"* (Mark 9:17-21, emphasis added).

Jesus asked the father, "How long has this been happening to him?" The response of the father is very interesting. The father replied, "From childhood." (v. 21). From childhood! The father's response makes many Christians uncomfortable. It troubles them to realize that even a small child can have a demon. This reality often does not fit neatly into many Christian's theological boxes that provide easy and simple answers to complex questions.

BREAKING DEMONIC BONDAGES IN CHILDREN

I am thankful that the Authority of the Believer is sufficient to break any demonic hold on a child, regardless of whether we have a logical explanation on how the demon spirit was able to get a foothold. As parents and church members, we need to pray for our children and the little ones that attend our churches because they are vulnerable. Satan does not fight fair and will attack the young, the vulnerable, and the weak. You could pray as follows:

> "Heavenly Father, I commit my children to you. I pray that one day they will accept your offer of a pardon. Until that day, I stand in the gap for my children. I take my spiritual authority which I have as I am 'seated in Christ' at your right hand and break all demonic strongholds in my children. I bind all demon spirits that may seek to attack or harm any of my children. I command that these demon spirits be sent to the pit."

THEORY OF DEMONIC BONDAGES ORIGINATING FROM GENERATIONAL SINS

I am going to discuss a popular theory on how demon spirits can afflict small children. My purpose for analyzing this theory is to try and minimize any confusion you may experience if you are exposed to this theory in the future. The theory that demon spirits can be transferred from past generations holds that individuals can have demonic bondages in their life, not only as a result of their personal unrepented sin but also because of the unrepented sins of past generations. Some believe that when a person dies and there is unrepented sin, the demon spirits carry the same characteristic of the particular sin to a person in the next generation. The main passage of Scripture used to support this theory is the Second Commandment:

> "You shall not make for yourself an idol, or any likeness of what is in heaven above or on the

earth beneath or in the water under the earth. You shall not worship them or serve them; for I, the Lord your God, am a jealous God, *visiting the iniquity of the fathers on the children, on the third and the fourth generations* of those who hate Me" (Exod. 20:4-5, emphasis added).

Some proponents of this theory state that the sins or sin bondages of the fathers can be passed down to the third and fourth generation. They argue it is actually the demon spirits who pass these sin bondages down to succeeding generations. This theory is supported by many Christian leaders, both charismatic and non-charismatic, who write books on spiritual warfare, and have information available on the internet about this issue.

Many of these leaders who support this theory have ministered to numerous individuals who were in bondage to demon spirits. Some of these Christian leaders claim that in deliverance sessions, the demon spirits have admitted they entered the person prior to birth and their "right" to enter was based on the sins of past generations. Some who hold this theory suggest that the person indwelt by these generational demon spirits is required to repent or renounce the sins of those in their past generations to break the demonic stronghold.[20]

RED FLAGS REGARDING THE EXISTENCE OF GENERATIONAL DEMONS

Most of the verses relied upon by those who believe in the theory of demonic involvement because of past unrepented generational sins are from the Old Testament. However, many of the promises and curses in the Old

Testament were made only to the Children of Israel and cannot be applied categorically to the church or individual believers. Yet, the principles found in the Old Testament do contain relevant principles for today. Care must be exercised when interpreting these verses. We need to keep these verses in their proper context. With context in mind, I would like to share a few red flags, or cautionary notes on this theory that should be considered.

Children are affected by the natural consequences of their parents' sin

It is self-evident that a person can be affected not only by his or her personal sins but also by the sins of others. Children can be affected by the natural consequences of the sins committed by their parents. For example, if a father is an alcoholic and refuses to provide for his family, his spouse and children will suffer. If a man commits adultery and later divorces his wife, the children obviously will be affected. However, these types of natural consequences of sin are not the result of God punishing the children for the sins of the parents. The children are actually the victims of the parents' sins.

There are Old Testament verses that state children can be affected by the sins of relatives in their past generations. "O Lord, in accordance with all Your righteous acts, let now Your anger and Your wrath turn away from Your city Jerusalem, Your holy mountain; for because of our sins and the iniquities of our fathers, Jerusalem and Your people *have become* a reproach to all those around us" (Dan. 9:16). Daniel and his generation were affected by the sins of their fathers. Daniel discerned that the wrath of God that came upon Jerusalem was in response, not only due to the sins of the current generation, but also because of "the iniquity" of the fathers; those in their past generations. The context of this passage reveals that the punishment of the Lord was coming upon the nation of Israel collectively because of past sins. On the other hand, the Book of Jeremiah clearly states that the sins of fathers can directly affect their children:

> "Ah Lord God! Behold, You have made the heavens and the earth by Your great power and by Your outstretched arm! Nothing is too difficult for You, who shows lovingkindness to thousands, *but repays the iniquity of fathers into the bosom of their children* after them, O great and mighty God. The Lord of hosts is His name" (Jer. 32:17-18, emphasis added).

This passage reveals that God "repays the iniquity of fathers into the bosom of their children." The meaning of "repays," however, is slightly ambiguous. At a minimum, it appears that the "consequences" of the sins of the fathers can affect children even before they are born. Also, the disciples, early in their ministry, exhibited a belief that sickness can be caused by a person's sin or even their parent's sin, most likely based on this and other Old Testament verses. "His disciples asked Him, 'Rabbi, who sinned, this man or his parents, that he would be born blind?' Jesus answered, '*It was* neither *that* this man sinned, nor his parents; but *it was* so that the works of God might be displayed in him'" (John 9:2-3). In this particular instance, Jesus stated that the blindness was not caused by his sin or his parents' sin.

Repenting of sins committed by others

Believers are not required to repent of sins committed by those in their past generations. My grandfather committed suicide. At the time, my grandmother was six months pregnant with my mother. This was a very evil act that my grandfather committed. However, I did not commit this sin. I am not personally responsible or accountable for my grandfather's sin. "The person who sins will die. The son will not bear the punishment for the father's iniquity, nor will the father bear the punishment for the son's iniquity" (Ezek. 18:20). This passage clearly states that God does *not* punish children for the sins of the fathers and was written by the prophet Ezekiel who was a contemporary of Jeremiah. So, when God states in Jeremiah 32:18 that He "repays the iniquity of fathers into the bosom of their children," based on what Ezekiel states here, we know that it means something other than God punishing children for the sins of the fathers when the children are completely innocent of the same sin.

Believers are shielded from God's wrath

Believers are no longer under the wrath of God because of the blood of Jesus Christ. "Much more then, having now been justified by His blood, we shall be saved from the wrath *of God* through Him" (Rom. 5:9). The Second Commandment states that God is "visiting the iniquity of the fathers on the children, on the third and the fourth generations." (Exod. 20:5). However, God is not visiting me for my sins (or because of my parents' sins), because I have been forgiven. I have been forgiven of my past, present, and even future sins. I am covered with the blood of

Jesus Christ, so God's wrath and His judgment passes over me. If you are a believer, the same is true of you.

If it were true that God is still visiting the sins of the fathers on the third and fourth generation, because the principle set forth in Exodus 20:5 is still applicable, we know that this curse is completely broken and destroyed at the time one receives Jesus Christ as Lord and Savior.[21] After you have accepted God's offer of a pardon, God is certainly not going to visit you for the sins of your parents or grandparents back to the third and fourth generation. This is a very important point to remember.

Information obtained from demon spirits

Much of the information that supports the theory that demon spirits can be transferred to succeeding generations was apparently learned by ministers during communication with demon spirits while trying to evict them from people.[22] These ministers argue that many people have found deliverance only after these generational demon spirits were confronted. However, experience is inherently unreliable. Other Christians must be able to independently evaluate the truth of any doctrine by relying on Scripture alone. I am not going to treat a belief or theory as doctrine and absolute truth when it allegedly came from a demon spirit, and cannot be independently verified from the Word of God.

Scriptures are silent on reality of generational spirits

There is nothing in Scripture that explicitly states demon spirits can use the sins of past generations to attack future generations. The Second Commandment states that "God visits the iniquity of fathers" on future generations.

It does not state that demons are being passed onto future generations because of the unrepented sins of past generations.[23] That is read into the text. Is it possible that when a person dies and there is unrepented sin, demon spirits can carry the same characteristic of that particular sin to a person in the next generation, which manifests as an enormous temptation to sin in a particular area? Yes, it is possible. There is nothing in Scripture that forecloses this possibility – but Scripture is silent.

I am not asserting that the Christian leaders who espouse this theory are wrong, but we cannot independently verify it based on the four corners of Scripture. If I own a boat, I want it secured by ropes and tied to the dock, so it does not just float away. In the same way, I want all of my beliefs about spiritual warfare to be securely fastened and tied to the Word of God. Nice theories on how the spiritual realms operate must remain as theories or personal convictions and not taught as absolute doctrinal truths. In eternity, God may explain many of the mysteries of the spiritual realms that are now the subject of human speculation. However, in the Church's quest for answers and explanations to difficult questions, care must be taken not to go beyond Scripture.

There is one thing we know with absolute certainty. Based on the authority of the Word of God, a demon spirit has no legal right to remain in a believer based on the sins of past generations. This is crystal clear! Fortunately, God has provided enough information in Scripture to be able to break any demonic bondage, regardless of how it came to be, even if it originates because of alleged past unrepented sins of deceased relatives and supposed generational demon spirits. Remember, our knowledge of the spiritual realms, as revealed in the Bible, is like the tip of an iceberg. Imagine if you could only see 3 percent of an iceberg and 97 percent was under the water and out of your sight. We understand far less than 3 percent of what transpires in the spiritual realms. But God knows everything. The Bible says that God knows the number of the stars and He gives names to them. God knows how demon spirits operate and how they attach to even small children. The Bible says that there is no creature hidden from His sight: "There is no creature hidden from His sight, but all things are open and laid bare to the eyes of Him with whom we have to do" (Heb. 4:13). The believer does not need in-depth knowledge of the spiritual realms, outside of Scripture, to break a demonic bondage.

I want to emphasize that it is not the believer's exhaustive knowledge of the spiritual realms that brings victory over Satan and his hosts but our faith in the Lord Jesus Christ. If this were not the case, the Bible would have provided more information on how demon spirits operate. As believers, we are to stand on the truth of the Word of God. First, God has forgiven us of all our sins through the blood of Jesus Christ. Second, our relationship with Satan has been severed. Third, we have authority in Christ to break all demonic bondages, regardless of their source.

AUTHORITY TO BREAK GENERATIONAL DEMONIC BONDAGES

God has provided a powerful weapon called the Authority of the Believer. In Chapter 10, I previously described that this authority is like a gun. I do not need to take a gun apart and understand how every part works to be able to use it. I just need to point it in the right direction and pull the trigger. God is just asking us to take the Authority of the Believer, point it at the powers of darkness, and pull the trigger by faith. "The seventy returned with joy, saying, 'Lord, even the demons are subject to us in Your name'… 'Behold, I [Jesus Christ] have given you authority to tread on serpents and scorpions, and over all the power of the enemy, and nothing will injure you" (Luke 10:17-19). God can break all demonic bondages regardless of its source.

If you have any concern that a demonic power has attached because of generational sins, abuse, trauma, or any other way, you might consider praying this prayer:

> "Heavenly Father, I take my spiritual authority which I have as I am 'seated in Christ' at your right hand, and I bind the demon spirits who have any stronghold in my life *regardless how such bondage originated*. I thank you that my relationship with Satan has been severed because of the blood of Christ. I command all demon spirits to leave me and go to the pit."

Remember, that after you exercise the Authority of the Believer and issue the command, it is God and the myriads of holy angels who enforce your authority. Once you issue the command, a battle begins in the spiritual realms. Some battles are won quickly, and others take time. Jesus Christ stated that certain demonic bondages are not broken instantly but only after prayer and fasting. Also remember in Daniel Chapter 10, it took the holy angel twenty-one days to break through the demonic blockade before reaching Daniel. In the same way, do not be discouraged if you do not see immediate results, but stand in faith that God is actively working to crush the powers of darkness in your life and in the lives of others whom you are praying for.

REMOVING DEMONIC STRONGHOLDS

At some point in your life, God may direct you to pray for and counsel a person who may have a demonic bondage. I will first share several important recommended steps when preparing to enter a spiritual battle. These steps should be taken prior to confronting the demons during a counselling session, if time permits. Preparation is the key to winning spiritual battles.

PREPARING FOR BATTLE

The first step is to ask God to reveal any unrepented sin in your life. Make sure that you are a clean vessel. Sin does not sever a believer's relationship with God, but it does hinder his or her fellowship and communion with God. Sin blocks the goodness of God and the power of the Holy Spirit. It will block your joy. It corrupts relationships. Unrepented sin is an open door to the powers of darkness to infiltrate your own life.

The second step is to surrender all areas of your life to the Holy Spirit and be filled with the Spirit. Check to make sure that every area of your life (every room) has been surrendered and yielded to the Holy Spirit. Ask God to fill you with the Holy Spirit. Make sure that you review the list of "Areas to Yield to the Holy Spirit" that is in the Appendix. You should prayerfully commit every area on the list to the Holy Spirit. Use the list as a starting point.

The third step is to ask God for protection. Ask God to have the holy angels protect you. Ask God to have the holy angels protect your family and loved ones. If Satan cannot harm you, he will try to harm those whom you love.

The fourth step is to put on each piece of the Armor of God. I have provided example prayers for putting on each piece of the Armor of God in the Appendix.

The fifth step is to pray that God would reveal any open door in the person's life. Pray that the person with the demonic bondage would be convicted of sin and become aware of any open door in their life that gave the demons power to create the bondage. The Sinventory in the Appendix that we discussed in Chapter 1 is a great tool to use. You should try to encourage the person to spend time in prayer, asking God to have the Holy Spirit convict and reveal unrepented sin in his or her life. This process can take weeks depending on the amount of unrepented sin. Often, as the person repents of the sin or sins, the demons leave and the bondage is removed, even without direct confrontation. Many individuals are delivered from demonic bondages by repentance alone; however, this is not always the case.

The sixth step is to pray that God would send the holy angels to weaken the demon spirits. Keep in mind, spiritual battles are usually won or lost prior to actually confronting the demons. So, ask God to weaken the demons who are creating the bondage. Also, remember that Jesus Christ said that certain kinds of demons can only be removed by prayer and fasting.

DIRECT CONFRONTATION

When the believer actually confronts a demon spirit in another person, during a formal counselling session, it is best to have at least one other believer present. If the person being ministered to is a woman, if possible, there should be a woman present who is a believer. This will protect the man in case the demon spirits in the woman try to create a situation to discredit or ruin the reputation of the man. This, of course, equally applies if a woman is ministering to a man, another man should be present.

One of the believers present should be in charge of talking to and commanding the demons. There should be one person in charge. Decide this issue up front. I do not recommend multiple people talking to and commanding the demons. This often creates confusion. The other believers who are present should silently pray as the Holy Spirit leads them, backing up the commands of the person who is in charge.

PRELIMINARY PRAYER REQUESTS

I recommend that you cover three specific areas in prayer with the person that you are counselling.

First, pray for wisdom and discernment. This is important because you may be confronted with perplexing and confusing circumstances in trying to break a demonic bondage. Thus, the believer should commit the whole process to God and ask for wisdom and discernment.

Second, pray for protection against the powers of darkness. The believer should pray for the physical, mental, emotional, and spiritual protection of the person indwelt by the demons and all of the participants. The believer should pray that everyone present would be covered by the blood of Jesus Christ and that their guardian angels would be present. The believer should pray that God would send additional angels to form a wall of fire around them. (Zech. 2:5).

Third, pray that God would have the holy angels surround the geographical area. I believe that demon spirits can travel with lightning speed across the earth. The believer should pray that God would send myriad upon myriads of holy angels. It is my conviction that this prayer creates a buffer zone which may prevent Satan from sending other demons from different parts of the world to assist the demons in the person who are trapped and are on the verge of being sent to the pit.

COMMANDS TO THE DEMON SPIRITS

The believer will next need to make three general commands to the demons. All commands to the demons should be made with the Authority of the Believer.

First, command the demon spirits not to speak unless you ask a question. If a demon manifests by using the person's vocal cords without being commanded to come up, the believer should command the demon "to go down" or "be quiet." The believer may need to be persistent with his authority and ask God to have the holy angels enforce this command. The demons may want to talk excessively to create a distraction.

Second, command the demons not to hurt the person when they leave. It is rare, but sometimes the demons will try to hurt the person when they leave, so this is important.

Third, command the demon spirits to go to the pit when they leave. Ask God to have the holy angels enforce this command and escort them to the pit. Do not let one of them escape.

KEY STEPS TO FREEDOM

There are five basic steps in breaking a spiritual bondage. The first step is to confirm that the person has accepted God's offer of a pardon. Even if the person claims they are saved, you should review the plan of salvation with them. You need to carefully confirm that each requirement for salvation has been met: admit, believe, and commit. There are many people who think they are saved just because they repeated a salvation prayer, attend a church, or were baptized. You need to carefully investigate whether the person has believed the Gospel, genuinely repented of their sin, and has surrendered to Jesus Christ as Lord of their life.

The second step is to identify all open doors in the person's life. Open doors include unrepented sin. Yet, I want to be clear that a demon spirit may have initially gained entrance to the person in ways other than unrepented sins such as abuse or a traumatic experience. As we discussed in Chapter 12, Scripture does not provide a complete list of all of the ways demons can gain access to a person. Also remember, there can be demons in the person that entered prior to salvation and have remained. When I use the term open door, I am generally referring to something that is under the control of the person (such as unrepented sin or deception) which if not dealt with upfront may allow other demons to return after the demons presently in the person are removed. However, I also recognize that a demon may have gained entrance through no fault of the person.

During the counselling session, even if the person indwelt by the demons has spent time beforehand trying to find the open doors (the ground), certain other sins will probably come to light as the Holy Spirit puts His searchlight on the person's heart. The person will need to repent of these sins. Often a demonic bondage will not be permanently removed unless the person has sincerely and thoroughly repented of all known sin because a door is still open. The goal is not only to get the demons out but to stay out. This requires, to the extent possible, that all doors that are open (which originally allowed the demons to gain entrance) must be closed. Thus, the majority of time in the counselling session will be spent in prayer with the person, as he or she repents of specific sin as God reveals the open doors.

Each area where a demonic bondage is suspected must be covered. For instance, sins of profanity, jealousy, pride, over-eating, negative thoughts, sexual immorality, arguments, bitterness, guilt, worry, occult practices, drugs, and violence all must be covered. Also, identify open doors of deception, including lies that the person has believed about himself, others, God, and Satan. The person will need to reject these lies in order to break the demonic stronghold. Also investigate whether the person has been involved in the occult, false religions, or may have pornographic or occult materials (*i.e.*, books, magazines, videos, etc.) in their home.

The third step in breaking a spiritual bondage is to take the Authority of the Believer and command that if there are any demon spirits within the person that they manifest and reveal their presence. Bringing your authority directly against the demon spirits will get their attention. You could pray as follows:

> "Heavenly Father, I take my spiritual authority, which I have as I am 'seated in Christ' at your right hand, and I bind the demon spirits that may be present in [Name of Person] and I command them to manifest and reveal their presence."

In some cases, the demons will respond to this command by using the person's vocal cords and will speak through the person. Most of the time they will not. In many instances, it is not actually necessary to command the demon to manifest. Manifestation of a demon is evidence to the person and the minister that the bondage they are experiencing is caused at least, in part, by a demon spirit. Thus, manifestation of a demon spirit is not always a necessary step for their removal.

The fourth step in breaking a spiritual bondage is to command the demons to leave. After all open doors have been identified and closed, the believer should exercise his or her authority and command the demons to leave and go to the pit. For example, the believer can pray:

> "Heavenly Father, I take my authority, which I have as I am 'seated in Christ' at your right hand, and I bind the demons spirits who are creating a bondage in the area of [specific sin, *i.e.*, unforgiveness, worry, lust, unbelief, anger, bitterness,

etc.] and I command them to leave and go to the pit."

You need to take this fourth step even if the demons did not manifest by taking over the person's vocal cords or manifesting in some other way. You must make all of your commands in faith and not rely on any physical manifestation to determine whether the demons have departed. Also, the believer should ask God to have the holy angels enforce his or her commands.

Commanding the demons to leave may remove the bondage instantaneously or gradually. I often wonder why God does not remove the demonic bondage immediately in all instances. In the Book of Daniel, Chapter 10, it took a holy angel twenty-one days to bring a message from God to the prophet Daniel. This is because the holy angel was blocked by a demon spirit for twenty-one days. There was a battle taking place in the spiritual realms. You may issue the command for the demons to leave, but once you do, there is a collision in the spiritual realms and a battle commences between the holy angels and the demons. Thus, the victory may be instantaneous or may take some time to achieve. Also, God may be teaching the person how to battle Satan in the spiritual realms. It is often the presence of a demonic bondage which will drive the person to prayer, repentance, study of the Word of God, and to come into a deeper trust and relationship with God. This is true even though with one word, God could break the demonic bondage immediately.

The fifth step in breaking a spiritual bondage is for the believer to ask that the Holy Spirit would fill the vacuum that is created after the demon spirit departs. It would appear that a spiritual vacuum is created when a demon spirit leaves a person:

> "When the unclean spirit goes out of a man, it passes through waterless places seeking rest, and does not find *it*. Then it says, *'I will return to my house from which I came'; and when it comes, it finds it unoccupied, swept, and put in order.* Then it goes and takes along with it seven other spirits more wicked than itself, and they go in and live there; and the last state of that man becomes worse than the first" (Matt. 12:43-45, emphasis added).

In this passage of Scripture, we do not know why the demon left the person. Apparently, the demon was not sent to the pit. If you follow my instructions, the demons that you remove from the person will be sent to the pit. They are never coming back, except possibly during the tribulation period (Rev. 9:1-4). However, other demons will attempt to exploit existing weaknesses to re-invade the person. Remember my illustration of the home with three bedrooms, two bathrooms, kitchen, and several other rooms that I discussed in Chapter 3. You need to have the person ask the Holy Spirit to fill that area of his life (the room) that was vacated when the demon left.

DEMONIC MANIFESTATIONS

In some instances, a demon spirit may manifest or reveal his presence. Manifestations come in a variety of forms. In a small number of cases, a demon spirit will be able to speak through the person. This type of manifestation will give direct evidence of the presence of a demon spirit. This is an objective manifestation. In the Bible, Jesus Christ encountered several demons who were able to use the vocal cords of a person:

> "Just then there was a man in their synagogue with an unclean spirit; and he cried out, saying, 'What business do we have with each other, Jesus of Nazareth? Have You come to destroy us? I know who you are–the Holy One of God!' And Jesus rebuked him, saying, 'Be quiet, and come out of him!'" (Mark 1:23-25).

In many cases, demon spirits will not be able to use the person's vocal cords. We are not certain why demons are able to use the vocal cords of some people but not others. It could be the level of passivity of the person toward the demon or the strength of the human will to resist such manifestation. Yet, a demon using a person's vocal cords is merely one type of manifestation that reveals the presence of a demon.

There can also be subjective manifestations that may give evidence of the demon's presence. There are instances where a person experiences a slight tightening around the throat. At other times, a person may experience increased anxiety when the Authority of the Believer is brought against the demon. Sometimes a person indwelt by the demons will be able to hear a voice in their mind on what the demons are saying in response to the believer's questions or commands. Other subjective manifestations include a sharp pain, a sudden fear (like they want to just get up and leave as quick as possible), or their heart may begin to race. It is very common for a person to notice a slight burp or yawn as the demon leaves. In Chapter 10, we discussed the difference between an objective manifestation and a subjective manifestation. I remind you that a subjective manifestation may be completely unrelated to a demonic presence.

In many cases, when a demon is bound and commanded to leave a person, there will be no physical manifestation. Often a demon will leave so quietly that the believer commanding the demon to leave will be unaware that it has departed. This is very common when the person has thoroughly repented of past sins and has closed all known doors to the powers of darkness. In that case, the demons are weak, defeated, trapped, surrounded by the holy angels, and provide little resistance. Even the person indwelt by the demon spirit will sometimes not be aware that the demon has gone, although the person will often sense a release in his or her mind or emotions. Warfare in the spiritual realms is by faith, not by sight.

SPEAKING WITH DEMON SPIRITS

Direct communication with demons must be approached with great caution. It is not forbidden to communicate with demons because it is evident from Scripture that Jesus Christ communicated with them. However, the believer is more susceptible to deception when directly communicating with a demon spirit. Remember, demon spirits have been around a long time. They have been watching humans for thousands of years. They are smarter than you. Your human knowledge and experience are no match for even the lowest ranking demon.

A demon can portray a variety of personalities. He may be submissive or aggressive. He may be talkative or very quiet. All demons have a distinct personality; however, they are also very good at deception and role playing. A demon may be very hostile. You should not believe any of the threats uttered from a demon. A demon may threaten to harm you or your family. You must realize that a demon cannot touch you or your family except by God's permission. Quoting Scripture at a demon is important when combating threats.

A demon may cry and beg for mercy. You should not yield to this deception. You are not to feel sorry for the demon or give him any sympathy. God has already condemned these forces to an eternity in the Lake of Fire for their rebellion. Presently, it is God's decision whether mercy is to be granted and not the believer's decision. You should not pity the demons. It is my conviction that in eternity God may delegate judgment of the demons to believers. There are verses that indicate believers will judge the angels (1 Cor. 6:3). This may include judging the fallen angels or demon spirits. Most likely with that authority will come the full knowledge of the relevant facts to determine whether mercy should be granted. But for now, show no mercy or pity to the demon spirits.

The demons may try to tempt the believer with pride. They may act afraid of you. They may state that you are specially chosen by God for an important task or far-reaching ministry. Completely disregard the demon's comments. Do not even consider them—lest you submit to the sin of pride or fall into deception and a door is opened in your life. Do not receive a compliment from a demon even if it is true. The demons do not give compliments to draw you closer to Jesus Christ. Instead, they are endeavouring to place a stumbling block before you. Any praise or call to a particular ministry should come from the Holy Spirit and not a demon.

The believer must not engage in unnecessary dialogue with the demons. When a demon spirit manifests, he may be very talkative. You must command the demon not to speak unless he is asked a question. Demon spirits are experts at lying and deceiving. The believer should resist the temptation to ask a question of a demon when the believer has not been led by the Holy Spirit. Most importantly, do not build a doctrine on demonic activity based on communication with demons. How foolish! Yet, many believers are engaging in this practice. There is a lot of misinformation based on what people have supposedly learned from demons while speaking with them.

I believe that it is not unreasonable to obtain the demon's name, when he entered the person, and the opened door (or sin ground) which permitted the demon to enter. As a general rule, however, questions directed to the demons should be kept at a minimum. In fact, it is not always necessary to ask the demon to identify the door which permitted him to enter the person. It is a better practice to initially question the person indwelt by the demon to find the open door. Obtaining a demon's name is permissible as seen in the Gospel of Mark but is not always necessary (Mark 5:9). In many instances, merely identifying and binding all demons who are creating the specific bondage and commanding them to leave is sufficient.

MAINTAINING YOUR FREEDOM

I would now like to discuss important steps to maintain your freedom. As I stated earlier, after the demons are removed, other demons will seek to move back in. The demons will pound on the doors to re-enter. Remember, the Apostle Paul said, "For our struggle is not against flesh and blood… " (Eph. 6:12). The person that you are counselling needs to take steps to maintain their freedom, so he or she does not become reinvaded.

Daily prayer

The first step to maintain your freedom is daily prayer. Let me ask a very honest question: In the last seven days, how many times did you quiet your heart and talk to God for at least five minutes? Frankly, many Christians do not pray each day. I would like to present a very practical and simple method to pray. It is called a 2 x 4 Quiet Time. I developed this method many years ago when I was teaching my children to pray. A copy of the Quiet Time form is in the Appendix. The 2 x 4 Quiet Time is an easy method to have a regular time of prayer each day. It is simple enough that a six-year-old can do it, but powerful enough to transform your life when used on a daily basis. It will take about five minutes.

Repentance of past sin

As you begin your quiet time, you need to deal with your past unrepented sins. Thus, you need to start out, "Dear God, I ask the Holy Spirit to convict me of any known sin in my life. I want to be pleasing to you." Why is this important? Of course, you should immediately repent after sinning. However, this prayer allows you to come before the Lord, once a day, and ask Him to reveal anything that you may have forgotten, or because of your busy schedule, you ignored. This prayer helps you to be a clean "vessel for honor." (2 Tim. 2:21). After you have taken a few moments to repent of your sins, then you are going to pray two prayers each in four categories.

Temptation

The first category is temptation. Ask God to strengthen you against two sins that you will probably be tempted to commit in the future. How do you know which two temptations to pray against? Just look how you stumbled and sinned within the last few days and pray against those temptations.

Praise

The second category is praise. Praise God for two things in your life. Regular praise results in an attitude adjustment. It makes you focus on the glass half full, not half empty. If you cannot think of anything to praise God about, let me give you a few suggestions:

1. Praise God that He is all powerful.
2. Praise God that He knows everything.
3. Praise God that no problem is too big or too small for Him to handle.
4. Praise God that He is in control of every circumstance in your life, even when you feel confused, fearful, or uncertain.
5. Praise God that He is in control when you are faced with a medical problem or financial problem.
6. Praise God that He will never leave you or forsake you in this life.

7. Praise God that your name is written in the Book of Life.

8. Praise God that He has forgiven you of all your sins.

9. Praise God that one day He will bring you to Heaven.

Also, remember to tell God regularly that you love Him with your whole heart.

Petition (prayer for yourself)

The third category is petition. Ask God to provide two needs or wants in your life. You should not assume that God will provide a need or a want if you did not ask Him. Do not be presumptuous. For example, if you are going to buy a car, and you have not asked God to give you wisdom or help, you should assume that you are on your own. But God wants to help you and give you wisdom. He wants to provide your needs.

You should not only ask God to provide your needs but also your wants. Praying for your wants is not always sinful. Just be careful to examine your motives. Many view God as a miser who will only give you a slice of stale moldy bread, just barely enough to sustain you. This is a lie. The truth is that God is gracious and often provides even our wants. For example, if you have been thinking about buying a house for years, bring that request before God. He might just say "Yes." Alternatively, by talking with God, He may change your heart where you are no longer constantly day-dreaming about buying that house. Also, be content if God answers "No" to your prayer request or reveals that you are to patiently wait for Him to grant the request in a different season.

Intercession (prayer for other people)

The fourth category is intercession. Ask God to meet a need or want for two other people. You need to regularly pray for friends, family members, and others to accept God's offer of a pardon, that is, to be saved. You need to be sensitive about the problems and concerns of other people. Praying for others takes your eyes off yourself. You also need to pray for your children by name. If you are not praying for your kids or grandkids, it is likely no one else is praying for them either, unless they have a godly Sunday school teacher.

In summary, when using the 2 x 4 Quiet Time method, you begin with repentance of past sins. Then you pray against two future temptations; offer two praises; make two requests for yourself (a need or a want); and pray for two other people. This should take about five minutes and will transform your life. It is a good starting point for developing your prayer life.

Read the Word of God

The second step to maintain your freedom is reading the Word of God. Your goal should be to read, at least, one chapter from the Bible each day. If you have not been doing so, start with the Gospel of John.

Fellowship with other believers

The third step to maintain your freedom is fellowship with other believers. God sometimes allows deficiencies in your life that only can be filled by other people. We win spiritual battles as a team. You need to join a team. Find a church and join it. All churches have flaws and problems. You will never find a perfect church. After you join it, select one ministry, and become actively involved. Do not just be a "pew sitter" or you will dry up and wither spiritually.

Share the Gospel

The fourth step to maintain your freedom is to share the Gospel. You need to regularly share the Gospel with people who need to hear the Good News. Regularly sharing the Gospel keeps you focused on fulfilling the Great Commission.

WARNINGS

There are some basic guidelines and warnings regarding spiritual warfare.

First, do not blame everything on demons. Do not give Satan credit for problems that he does not cause. Some problems that will come into your life are unrelated to demon spirits.

Second, all disease and sickness are not caused by demons. In some instances, physical infirmities can be caused by demons but not all. Physical illness that is unrelated to demonic activity may be experienced by Holy Spirit-filled believers.

Third, a person can have a mental challenge or illness and not have a demon. We live in an evil world. Wicked influences surround us every day. The human mind can be affected not only by demon spirits, but also by an individual's genetics, past trauma, abuse, life experiences, family background, and environment among others.[24] Thus, mental challenges are not always a result of a direct demonic assault or demonic in origin.

Fourth, just because the believer has not repented of a particular sin does not mean the believer has a demon residing in him or her. The presence of sin in the believer's life does not necessarily mean the presence of a demon.

Fifth, the rebuking of a demon spirit in a person should never be sensationalized. The minister's primary objective is to help the person under the demonic bondage to be delivered. It is not to create a show to impress other believers or lost people with your authority over the demon spirits. Do not fall into the temptation of stealing the glory that belongs only to the Lord Jesus Christ.

There are factors to consider whether deliverance should take place in a public or private setting. There are situations where a demon spirit can and should be removed without any pre-counseling steps. For example, there were no pre-counseling steps in the Gospel of Mark when Jesus Christ rebuked the unclean spirit in the man at a synagogue. (Mark 1:23-27). In other instances, the rebuking of a demon spirit in public without adequate counseling may not provide permanent victory over the powers of darkness, especially if there are numerous open doors that need to be closed. This could give the person indwelt by the demons and others in the audience a misunderstanding of what just transpired, especially if all of the demons are not removed. The goal is to achieve long term victory over the powers of darkness and not merely a sensational encounter which gives the appearance of victory.

Practically speaking, it often takes significant time to identify and shut the open doors which gave the demons access to the person. Addressing these open doors may not be feasible in a service where there are time constraints and several people are seeking deliverance. If demons are removed, but doors are still open, other demons might be able to reinvade the person. Thus, any victory could be short lived. Wisdom should be exercised in each unique circumstance on whether deliverance should be held in public because it often takes time to identify the open doors. Also, God does not demand that all sins need to be confessed publicly. Exposing the person's sins publicly can unnecessarily embarrass the person. Always focus on the best interest of the person seeking help.

Sixth, test all teachings on spiritual warfare by the Word of God. There exists a lot of misinformation on spiritual warfare that is hindering the church's effectiveness in combating and defeating Satan and his hosts. Do not believe everything you hear or read regarding spiritual warfare and deliverance. You must test everything. This includes every word you have read in this book as well as other teachings.

APPENDIX

SPIRITUAL
WARFARE

Plea Agreement

The below-mentioned person desires to enter into a Plea Agreement with GOD THE FATHER, Creator of Heaven and Earth, in full and final settlement of the charge. The effect of entering this Plea Agreement will grant the person a pardon from the penalty of all their sin. Prior to entering or signing this Plea Agreement, a person is cautioned to carefully examine his or her heart and motives and consider the costs. This Plea Agreement shall be void and have no legal effect should the person not commit to each and every one of the pardon conditions set forth below.

I. THE CHARGE
YOU HAVE SINNED AGAINST GOD.

"For all have sinned and fall short of the glory of God" (Rom. 3:23).

II. THE PENALTY
THE PENALTY OF THE CHARGE
IS ETERNAL PUNISHMENT.

"The wages of sin is death…" (Rom. 6:23).

"These will go away into eternal punishment, but the righteous into eternal life" (Matt. 25:46).

III. THE PARDON

GOD THE FATHER has offered a complete and absolute pardon to the charge upon the below-mentioned person agreeing and committing to the following conditions:

A. *Pardon Condition No. 1 - Admit*

I plead guilty to the charge and admit that I have sinned against God by my actions, words, and thoughts.

B. *Pardon Condition No. 2 - Believe*

1. I believe that the penalty of my sin is eternal punishment.

2. I believe that Jesus Christ is the Son of God and that He died on a cross and shed His blood to pay the penalty for my sin. I believe that He was buried and arose from the dead on the third day.

C. *Pardon Condition No. 3 - Commit*

1. I confess that Jesus Christ is Lord and submit and surrender to Him as the absolute boss and authority of my life.

2. I repent of all my sins and ask God for His forgiveness. I also ask God for His grace and help that I might turn from all my sin.

I personally accept the pardon by faith upon understanding and fulfilling these conditions.

Dated: _____   _____
                                                Signature

Witness: _____

"In the hope of eternal life, which God, who cannot lie, promised long ages ago" (Titus 1:2).

"For God so loved the world, that He gave His only begotten Son, that whoever believes in Him shall not perish, but have eternal life" (John 3:16).

KUGLER SCHOOL OF

SPIRITUAL
WARFARE

AREAS TO SURRENDER TO THE HOLY SPIRIT

The believer should submit and surrender every area of his or her life (rooms in the believer's house) to the Holy Spirit including, but not limited to, the following areas:

Past hurts

Future dreams and goals

Family

Thought life

Time

Church involvement

Finances

Offerings

Material possessions

Relationships

Attitude toward spouse or parents

Fears

Tongue

Self-Esteem

Pride

Sexuality

Health

Eating habits

Job and/or school

Talents and gifts

Evangelistic opportunities

Relaxation and entertainment

Will

Emotions

"You will seek Me and find Me when you search for Me with all your heart" (Jer. 29:13);

"Submit therefore to God. Resist the devil and he will flee from you" (Jam. 4:7).

SPIRITUAL
WARFARE

COMMON LIES

The Belt of Truth of the Armor of God protects the believer from four types of lies: (1) lies about God, (2) lies about yourself, (3) lies about others, and (4) lies about Satan.

LIES ABOUT GOD

Satan tempts Christians and others to believe lies about God. Satan sometimes adds a little truth to help a person more easily swallow the lie. Some of the common lies that you should reject include:

1. "God will not forgive you of certain sins such as homosexuality, child abuse, rape, adultery, suicide, murder, divorce, and incest."

2. "God will only continue to love you if you stop sinning."

3. "There will be no consequences if you sin against God because you are under grace."

4. "God is punishing you for your past sins whenever you get sick."

5. "God cannot be trusted with your finances, employment, or health. You had better take care of yourself because God may drop the ball."

6. "God only cares about Himself. He is a user. He brings painful and confusing circumstances into your life just to bring glory to Himself, but cares little about you or your problems."

7. "God is really not all powerful. God brags about His power in the Bible but cannot deliver on promises. He requires you to 'wait' and 'walk by faith' as an excuse for His lack of power to deliver on His promises."

8. "God is mean-spirited. If God is truly all powerful but does not help you, it shows that He really does not care."

9. "All religions lead to God if a person is sincere in his belief."

10. "You have committed the unforgiveable sin by blaspheming the Holy Spirit."

The believer should pray, "Lord, show me lies that I have believed about You."

LIES ABOUT YOURSELF

You must reject lies about yourself that Satan directs into your mind. Some of the common lies that you should reject include:

1. "You are not smart enough to study or understand the Bible."

2. "You will fail in all future business endeavors. You are a failure!"

3. "You are not entitled to be loved by God and others. Who could love you?"

4. "You will never overcome certain sins or harmful habits."

5. "You will get cancer or some other disease when there is no rational basis to believe so."

6. "You have no ability to share the Gospel. You will cause more harm than good."

7. "You are ugly, stupid, and worthless. No one would want to be your friend."

The believer should pray, "Lord, show me lies that I have believed about myself."

LIES ABOUT OTHERS

Too often, believers misinterpret the words or actions of other people and draw false conclusions. This improper behavior is a barrier to developing healthy relationships. It can also produce unjustified bitterness or anger. Lies about others affect friendships, family members, and ministry partners. Satan knows that you are far more vulnerable if you are isolated. Thus, Satan's goal is to place wedges in your relationships by planting lies. You may believe these lies (or similar lies) about another person, or someone may believe these lies about you, which can also be very painful. Some of the common lies that you should reject include:

1. "Another person hates you, when they do not."

2. "Your spouse has or wants to cheat on you, when he or she does not."

3. "Another person is critical of your appearance and judging you, when they are not."

4. "Another person is prejudiced toward you because of your race or financial status and is looking down his or her nose at you, when they are not."

5. "Another person made a sexual advance toward you, when that person did not."

6. "Another person is full of pride, when they are not."

Obviously, in some cases you may be correct in your perception of what the other person is thinking. If this is true, you will still need God's grace. This is why believers are to be patient with all people. We are not to take into account a wrong suffered. Yet, often the believer has merely swallowed a lie and is only speculating on how another person is thinking.

The believer should pray, "Lord, show me the lies that I have believed about others and break the lies that people believe about me."

LIES ABOUT SATAN

There are many Christians who claim to believe the Bible but deny some fundamental truths it reveals about Satan. A Christian cannot be effective in spiritual warfare if he or she has believed lies about Satan. Believing lies about Satan can weaken your faith in God. Some of the common lies that you should reject include:

1. "Satan does not exist but is a myth or merely a symbol of evil."

2. "Demon spirits cannot develop a bondage in a believer's life, even if he or she indulges in habitual sin and fails to repent."

3. "Hell does not exist or is not eternal."

4. "Satan is more powerful than God."

5. "All demonic bondages are always broken at the time of salvation."

The believer should pray, "Lord, show me lies that I have believed about Satan."

TRUTH STATEMENTS

Once a person has accepted God's offer of a pardon, it is important to put on the Belt of Truth and accept the truth about your new relationship with God:

1. God truly loves and cares for me.

2. God is trustworthy, faithful, and always keeps His promises.

3. God is with me and will never desert me.

4. God can help me and give me wisdom.

5. God has compassion and mercy on me.

6. I have been forgiven of all my sins.

7. I have been given eternal life and a place in Heaven is reserved for me.

8. I have been adopted by God as His child.

9. God does not condemn me even when I stumble and sin against Him.

10. The Holy Spirit can give me the power to overcome sinful habits and addictions.

11. When God looks upon me, He sees the very righteousness of Jesus Christ.

12. God knew me before the foundations of the world, and He chose to have a relationship with me even though He knew all my faults.

13. God has a plan for my life that was formed in eternity past.

14. God can accomplish His will in my life, even without me knowing all of the steps that need to be taken to accomplish His will.

15. God is using the difficult circumstances in my life for my good and His glory.

16. God understands the pain and confusion of my heart.

17. God has given me all the talents, gifts, and resources that I need to fulfill His plan for my life.

18. Any deficiency I have can be filled by other people that God will bring into my life or directly by God Himself.

19. Satan and his hosts have already been defeated when Jesus Christ died on the cross, shed His blood, paid the penalty for my sin, and arose from the dead.

20. God's Word is powerful and is as a sword (dagger) against the powers of darkness to overcome temptation in my life.

21. I have authority over the powers of darkness because I am "seated in Christ" at God's right hand in the heavenly places.

22. All the powers of darkness who have invaded my life are subject to my will and are merely trespassers, squatters, and have no legal right to remain and must leave.

23. God is almighty, all powerful, unstoppable, and there is none who can deliver out of His hand.

24. The holy angels watch over me day and night and are battling the demon spirits who are tempting me, trying to deceive me, and seeking to obtain a stronghold in my life.

25. The powers of darkness tremble and are in anguish because of God's great name and power.

KUGLER SCHOOL OF

SPIRITUAL WARFARE

Blasphemy against the Holy Spirit

The lie that a person has committed the "blasphemy against the Holy Spirit" is so prevalent it merits an explanation. It seems that Satan tries this lie on every Christian at least one time. Satan's strategy is ordinarily to confuse the believer on how this sin is actually committed. The Gospel of Mark describes this sin:

> "The scribes who came down from Jerusalem were saying, 'He is possessed by Beelzebul,' and 'He casts out the demons by the ruler of the demons.' And he [Jesus] called them to Himself and began speaking to them in parables, 'How can Satan cast out Satan?'… 'Truly I say to you, all sins shall be forgiven the sons of men, and whatever blasphemies they utter; but whoever blasphemes against the Holy Spirit never has forgiveness, but is guilty of an eternal sin" – because they were saying, 'He has an unclean spirit'" (Mark 3:22-23 and Mark 3:28-30).

The blasphemy against the Holy Spirit is not committing suicide, genocide, murder, incest, rape, or child molestation. These are obviously terrible sins but clearly forgivable. The blasphemy against the Holy Spirit is also not merely rejecting the Gospel message because a person can reject Jesus Christ earlier in his life, but years later repent and receive Jesus Christ as Lord and Savior and be forgiven. Some might suggest that if a person rejects the Gospel and dies that this is an unforgivable sin. I agree. However, I do not think this is what Jesus Christ is referring to in the Gospel of Mark as the blasphemy of the Holy Spirit, based on the context of Scripture.

In the Gospel of Mark, Jesus warned the scribes about the blasphemy against the Holy Spirit *"because they were saying, 'He has an unclean spirit'"* (Mark 3:29). In other words, the scribes observed Jesus Christ perform a miracle (casting out a demon), but they attributed the miracle to Satan. Thus, the sin of blasphemy against the Holy Spirit appears to be knowingly and willfully attributing a clear work of the Holy Spirit to Satan. Some might assert that this sin could only be committed by a person who: (1) actually witnessed a miracle performed by Jesus Christ, (2) knew it was a true miracle from God and (3) attributed the miracle to Satan. There is a strong argument that this sin can no longer be committed because Jesus Christ is no longer physically present on the earth.

Even assuming this sin can still be committed, the required conditions for a person to commit this sin are seldom present. This sin is not committed when the believer makes a mistake in judgment or lashes out at God in anger from a confused or wounded heart. In order to commit this sin, a person would have to (1) believe a true miracle was performed, (2) know the miracle was produced by the

Holy Spirit, and (3) then intentionally attribute the miracle to Satan. Furthermore, when a person actually commits this sin, the person's heart becomes hardened because the Holy Spirit no longer brings conviction of sin. The Holy Spirit is quenched and no longer operates in the person's life. *A person who has committed this eternal sin does not even worry or care that he or she has sinned against God.*

The important point to remember is that a person who has the slightest concern about the possibility of having committed this sin, seeks forgiveness, or still loves God, is revealing unquestionable proof that he or she has not blasphemed the Holy Spirit. Believers should stop accepting this destructive lie.

Bruce A. Kugler
Bruce Kugler Ministries

SPIRITUAL
WARFARE

Quiet Time Form
2 x 4

"Dear God, as I begin my quiet time, I ask the Holy Spirit to convict me of any sin in my life. I want to be pleasing to You."

TEMPTATION

Ask God to strengthen you against two sins that you may be tempted to commit.

1. _____

2. _____

Example: "Dear God, I pray against the sin of bitterness. I know that when I am with _____ today, I will be tempted with bitterness because of things that happened in the past. Please give me strength so that I will not yield to this sin today."

PRAISE

Praise God for two things in your life.

1. _____

2. _____

Example: "Dear God, I praise you for my family."

PETITION

(A personal petition is requesting God for a need or want in your life)

Ask God for two needs or wants in your life.

1. _____

2. _____

Example: "Dear God, I pray for a job. I ask that you open up the door so I can have a job to provide for my family and one that will honor you."

INTERCESSION

(Intercession is requesting God for a need or want for another person)

Ask God to meet a need or want for two other people.

1. _____

2. _____

Example: "Dear God, I pray for my pastor. I pray that You would give him wisdom to lead our church."

SPIRITUAL
WARFARE

SUGGESTED PRAISES

1. Praise God that He is all powerful.

2. Praise God that He knows everything.

3. Praise God that no problem is too big or too small for Him to handle.

4. Praise God that He is in control of every circumstance in your life, even when you feel confused, fearful, or uncertain.

5. Praise God that He is in control when you are faced with a medical or a financial problem.

6. Praise God that He is with you and will never leave you or abandon you.

7. Praise God that your name is written in the Book of Life.

8. Praise God that He has forgiven you of all your sin.

9. Praise God that one day He will bring you to Heaven.

10. Tell God that you love Him with your whole heart.

"Why am I discouraged? Why is my heart so sad? I will put my hope in God! I will Praise him again—my Savior and my God!" (Ps. 42:5-6 NLT); "I call upon the Lord, who is worthy to be praised, And I am saved from my enemies" (Ps. 18:3); "Praise Him for His mighty deeds; praise Him according to His excellent greatness" (Ps. 150:2).

SPIRITUAL
WARFARE

Example Prayers for Spiritual Warfare

CHAPTER 1 – BREAKING SIN BONDAGES

Prayer for salvation

"God, I admit that I have sinned. I believe the penalty of my sin is eternal punishment. I believe that Your son Jesus Christ died on a cross, shed his blood to pay the penalty for my sin, and arose from the dead. I commit my life to Jesus Christ. I submit to Jesus Christ as the absolute boss and authority of my life. I repent of my sin. I confess Jesus Christ as my Lord. I accept Your offer of a pardon by faith." *See* Rom. 3:23, Rom. 6:23, John 3:16, Rom. 10:9, Luke 13:5, and Eph. 2:8-9.

Prayer for God to reveal past unrepented sins

"Heavenly Father, I pray that You would put Your search-light on my heart and bring to my mind sins that I have committed in the past but have never repented of. I want to make sure that all doors that I have opened to the powers of darkness through my unrepented sin are now closed." *See* Ps. 139:23.

Prayer of repentance

"Heavenly Father, I repent of _____. I turn from this sin. I thank You for the forgiveness that I have because Jesus Christ shed His blood on the cross. Thank You for cleansing me from this sin. I close the door to the powers of darkness." *See* 1 John 1:9.

CHAPTER 2 – THE BATTLEGROUND

Prayer for protection from the evil one

"Heavenly Father, I praise You that You love me. I praise You that when I accepted Your offer of a pardon that You transferred me from the Kingdom of Satan to the Kingdom of God. I praise You that I am now a member of Your family. I pray that You would protect me and my family from the evil one." *See* John 17:15, Col. 1:13, Ps. 23:4, and 2 Tim 4:18.

Prayer against worldliness

"Heavenly Father, I pray against worldliness in my life. I ask that You help me to avoid worldly influences that tempt me to sin against You. I pray that You will help me to love and care for people who do not know You but not to become involved with their sinful activities. Give me wisdom on relationships with other people. I pray against the love of money and the desire for worldly possessions. I pray against the desire for fame and recognition. Finally, I pray against my lust for power, acting bossy, and always wanting to tell people what to do." *See* 1 John 2:15-17 and Matt. 20:25-28.

CHAPTER 3 – FULLNESS OF THE HOLY SPIRIT

Prayer to be filled with the Holy Spirit

"Heavenly Father, I have repented of all known past sins. I have closed the doors to the powers of darkness in my life. I now surrender every area in my life (every room in my house) to the Holy Spirit. Specifically, I yield the area of _____ to the Holy Spirit. I give You permission to clean and remodel this room. I pray and claim in faith that I would be filled with the Holy Spirit." *See* Eph. 5:18 and 2 Cor. 5:7.

CHAPTER 4 – OVERCOMING TEMPTATION

Prayer to reject the lie that a believer has no power to resist temptation

"Heavenly Father, I reject the lie that I have no power to resist temptation. I thank You that my sin nature was crucified with Christ on the cross and I no longer have to be controlled and dominated by sin. I praise You that I no longer have to be controlled by the sin of _____." *See* Rom. 6:6 and 1 Cor. 10:13.

Prayer to be dead to sin

"Heavenly Father, I claim that I am 'dead to the sin' of _____. I pray that You would deaden my desire to give into temptations that are presented to my mind. I pray that I would not give into temptation. As a dead person would not respond to a pin pricking his hand, so I pray that I would be as a dead man to the pin prick of temptation." *See* Rom. 6:11.

Prayer for strength in your will to resist temptation

"Heavenly Father, I acknowledge that I cannot in my own strength overcome all sinful temptations. Yet, I know my will is involved in this process. I pray that You will give me supernatural strength in my will to resist and reject sinful temptations." *See* Phil. 2:13, 1 Cor. 10:13, and Gen. 4:7.

Prayer to reject sinful thoughts

"Heavenly, Father, I reject this thought of _____." *See* 2 Cor. 10:5 and Phil. 4:8.

CHAPTER 5 – THE ARMOR OF GOD

Prayer against false doctrine

"Heavenly Father, I put on the Belt of Truth. I pray that You would reveal any misunderstanding that I have in doctrine or practice regarding the Word of God. Please reveal all lies and deception in my life." *See* Eph. 6:14 and 2 Tim. 4:3.

Prayer against lies

"Heavenly Father, I put on the Belt of Truth. Please show me the lies that I have believed about myself, other people, You, and Satan." *See* Eph. 6:14 and John 8:44.

Prayer against guilt

"Heavenly Father, I put on the Breastplate of Righteousness. I thank You that I have been forgiven of all my past, present, and future sins. I thank You that there is no condemnation for those who have accepted Your offer of a pardon. I thank You that when You look upon me, You see that I am clothed with the very righteousness of Jesus Christ." *See* Rom. 5:17, Rom. 10:9-10, Rom. 8:1, and Phil. 3:9.

Prayer to share the Gospel

"Heavenly Father, I put on the Gospel Shoes. I pray that You would help me be prepared to share the Gospel with anyone that You bring across my path today. I pray that You would grant me boldness and confidence." *See* Eph. 6:15, 1 Pet. 3:15, and Eph. 6:19.

Prayer for the peace of God

"Heavenly Father, I put on the Gospel Shoes of Peace. I thank You that the Holy Spirit can give me the peace of God when turmoil and trials come into my life. I claim the peace of God in the situation of _____." *See* Eph. 6:15, John 14:27, and John 16:33.

Prayer when reading and meditating on the Word of God

"Heavenly Father, as I begin to read and meditate on the Word of God, I thank You that the unfolding of Your Word gives light and is like a hammer that smashes a rock. Your Word is powerful. I pray that Your Word would be as light and fire as it comes into my mind and would increase my faith. I pray that You would push out all of the powers of darkness that are within me and break all demonic strongholds in my life. I pray that I would be filled with Your presence and the power of the Holy Spirit." *See* Ps. 119:130, Jer. 23:29, and Eph. 5:18.

Prayer against doubt

"Heavenly Father, I take up the Shield of Faith. I thank You that I can trust in the promises that You have made in Your Word. I praise You that You are always with me and will never desert me. I praise You that You can help me and give me wisdom. I reject all thoughts that tempt me to doubt Your Word, Your goodness, Your existence, Your power, Your plan for my life, and Your great love for me. I praise You that You are trustworthy, faithful, and always keep Your promises." *See* Eph. 6:16, Rom. 10:17, Gen. 28:15, Isa. 41:10, Gen. 3:1-5, Jam. 1:5, and Heb. 13:5.

Prayer for when a crisis comes into your life

"Heavenly Father, I take up the Shield of Faith. I give You the fear and uncertainty that I am feeling. I thank You that You are always in control even when I am not in control. I thank You that nothing can come into my life without going through Your divine filter. I praise You that You are with me in this situation. I know that You love me. I will trust You and obey You even though I do not understand why You have allowed this circumstance to come into my life." *See* Eph. 6:16, Ps. 103:19, Deut. 29:29, and Isa. 41:10.

Prayers for using the Word of God as a sword against temptation

Fear

"Heavenly Father, I reject this thought of <u>fear</u>. 'When I am afraid I will trust in You.'" *See* Ps. 56:3.

Quarreling

"Heavenly Father, I reject this thought of <u>quarreling</u>. 'The Lord's bond-servant must not be quarrelsome.'" *See* 2 Tim. 2:24.

Revenge

"Heavenly Father, I reject this thought of <u>revenge</u>. 'Never take your own revenge.'" *See* Rom. 12:19.

Sexual lust

"Heavenly Father, I reject this thought of <u>sexual lust</u>. 'Now flee from youthful lusts.'" *See* 2 Tim. 2:22.

Swearing

"Heavenly Father, I reject this thought of <u>swearing</u>. 'Let no unwholesome word proceed from your mouth.'" *See* Eph. 4:29.

Lying

"Heavenly Father, I reject this thought of <u>lying</u>. 'Do not lie to one another.'" *See* Col. 3:9.

Worry

"Heavenly Father, I reject this thought of <u>worry</u>. 'Be anxious for nothing.'" *See* Phil. 4:6.

Selfishness

"Heavenly Father, I reject this thought of <u>selfishness</u>. 'Do nothing from selfishness.'" *See* Phil. 2:3.

Grumbling

"Heavenly Father, I reject this thought of <u>grumbling</u>. 'Do all things without grumbling.'" *See* Phil. 2:14.

Coveting

"Heavenly Father, I reject this thought of <u>coveting</u>. 'You shall not covet.'" *See* Exod. 20:17.

Vain Imagination

"Heavenly Father, I reject this thought of <u>vain imagination</u>. 'Turn away my eyes from looking at vanity.'" *See* Ps. 119:37.

Doubt

"Heavenly Father, I reject this thought of <u>doubt</u>. 'But he must ask in faith without any doubting.'" (Jam. 1:6).

Unbelief

"Heavenly Father, I reject this thought of <u>unbelief</u>. 'With respect to the promise of God, he did not waver in unbelief'" (Rom. 4:20).

CHAPTER 6 – HOLY ANGELS

Praise God that holy angels will bring you to Heaven

"Heavenly Father, I thank You that I do not need to be afraid of death. I praise You that You are always with me, and I can have Your peace. I thank You that Your holy angels will be with me when the Lord Jesus Christ himself brings me to Heaven." *See* Luke 16:22 and Ps. 23:4.

Praise God that holy angels are guarding you

"Heavenly Father, I praise You that You have assigned holy angels to guard me in all my ways. I praise You that the holy angels are powerful." *See* Ps. 91:11 and Ps. 103:19-20.

Prayer to have holy angels battle demon spirits

"Heavenly Father, I pray that You would have the holy angels surround me and protect me against the demon spirits who are tempting, deceiving, and attacking me. I pray that You would have the holy angels execute Your fierce wrath and judgment against the demon spirits and destroy them." *See* Ps. 91:11, 2 Kings 6:15-17, Dan. 10:12-13, Rev. 12:7, Mark 1:24, and Matt. 26:53.

CHAPTER 7 – BLOOD OF JESUS CHRIST

Praise God that you have direct access

"Heavenly Father, I praise You that I have direct access to You because Jesus Christ shed His blood on the cross, paid the penalty for my sin, and arose from the dead. I thank You that I can talk directly to You and You hear my every thought. I thank You that You love me and want to intervene on my behalf and help me with the problems that I face in this life." *See* Heb. 10:19, Eph. 2:18, and Eph. 3:12.

Prayer to plead the blood of Jesus Christ

"Heavenly Father, I plead the blood of Jesus Christ as a reminder to the powers of darkness of what You have done for me through the shedding of Jesus Christ's precious blood on the cross. I thank You that I have been forgiven of my sins. I thank You that You purchased me with the blood of Jesus Christ. I acknowledge that You own me and everything that I possess. I thank You that my relationship with Satan was completely severed when I accepted Your offer of a pardon." *See* Heb. 9:22, Rev. 1:5, Acts 20:28, and Col. 1:13.

CHAPTER 8 – SATAN AND HIS FALLEN ANGELS

Prayer against fear of Satan

"Heavenly Father, I praise You that when Jesus Christ died on the cross and shed His blood to pay the penalty of sin and was resurrected three days later, Satan and all of the demon spirits were completely defeated. Not only have they been defeated, but they have been disarmed. I praise You that the Holy Spirit who resides in me, is far greater and more powerful than Satan." *See* Col. 2:15 and 1 John 4:4.

Prayer for preventing Satan from obtaining three weapons

"Heavenly Father, I praise You that Satan has been defeated and disarmed. Now that Satan has been disarmed, the only weapons that Satan can use against me are the ones that I personally give to him. Do not let Satan deceive me by giving him weapons because I know that he will use them against me." *See* Col. 2:15, 2 Cor. 2:11, and Eph. 4:27.

Satan's first weapon: Power of sin

"Heavenly Father, I pray that I would not give Satan the weapon of the 'power of sin' because I know that he will use this weapon against me. I put on the Breastplate of Righteousness. I pray that You would show me any unrepented sin in my life. I pray that Satan would not have any access to my life through open doors because of unrepented sin. I repent of _____." *See* Eph. 4:27, Ps. 139:23-24, 1 John 1:9, Rom. 6:14-15, and Isa. 59:1-2.

Satan's second weapon: Deception

"Heavenly Father, I pray that I would not give Satan the weapon of 'deception' because I know that he will use this weapon against me. I put on the Belt of Truth. I ask the Holy Spirit to reveal any lies and deception in my life. I ask that You destroy all lies that I believe about the Bible, myself, others, You, and Satan." *See* John 8:44, Eph. 4:27, 2 Tim. 4:3, and Eph. 6:14.

Satan's third weapon: Fear of persecution

"Heavenly Father, I pray that I would not give Satan the weapon of the 'fear of persecution' (fear of man) because I know that he will use this weapon against me and attempt to manipulate and control me. I thank You that Satan cannot lay one finger on my life without obtaining Your permission. I fully surrender my life to Jesus Christ. I pray

that I would love You more than I love even my own life."
See Rev. 2:10, Job 1:9-12, and Rev. 12:11.

CHAPTER 9 – AUTHORITY OF THE BELIEVER

Prayer against temptation

"Heavenly Father, I take my spiritual authority which I
have as I am 'seated in Christ' at Your right hand and I
bind the demon spirit who is interjecting this thought of
_____ into my mind. I command this demon
spirit to leave and go to the pit." *See* 1 Thess. 3:5, Eph. 2:6,
2 Cor. 10:5, and Matt. 16:19.

Prayer for a person to accept God's offer of a pardon

"Heavenly Father, I pray that _____ would
hear and understand the Gospel. I pray that they would be
convicted of their sin and understand that You are a holy
and righteous God. I pray that You would convict them
that there will be a judgment day in which everyone will
be held accountable for their sins. I pray that they would
believe the Gospel that Jesus died on a cross to pay the
penalty for sin and arose from the dead. I pray that they
would accept Your offer of a pardon." *See* Rom. 10:14, John
16:8, Rom. 10:10, and John 3:16.

Prayer against Satan who is blinding a person from seeing their need for a savior

"Heavenly Father, I take my spiritual authority, which I
have as I am 'seated in Christ' at your right hand, and I
pray that all of the demon spirits, who are blinding and
hindering _____from understanding the

Gospel and seeing their need to accept Your offer of a pardon, would be bound and the demons' attacks would cease." *See* 2 Cor. 4:3-4, Eph. 2:6, and Matt. 16:19.

Prayer against Satan who would try and steal the Word of God

"Heavenly Father, I take my spiritual authority, which I have as I am 'seated in Christ' at Your right hand, and I pray that You would bind the demon spirits who will try to steal the Word of God from people's hearts and minds to hinder them from accepting Your offer of a pardon." *See* Matt. 13:19, Eph. 2:6, and Matt. 16:19.

Prayer against Satan who would try and thwart a ministry

"Heavenly Father, I take my spiritual authority, which I have as I am 'seated in Christ' at Your right hand, and I pray that You would bind the demon spirits who are trying to thwart and prevent this ministry from being established. I pray that You would send Your holy angels to enforce my authority, to destroy the demon spirits, and take them to the pit." *See* 1 Thess. 2:18, Eph. 2:6, and Matt. 16:19.

Prayer to remove demonic bondage in the believer's life

"Heavenly Father, I have repented of _____. I have closed the door to the powers of darkness in my life. I now take my spiritual authority, which I have as I am 'seated in Christ' at Your right hand, and I bind the demon spirits who have created this spiritual bondage in my life, and I command them to leave and go to the pit." *See* Acts 16:16-18, Eph. 2:6, and Matt. 16:19.

CHAPTER 10 – HOW DEMONS AFFECT THE BELIEVER

Praise God that the believer can never be possessed (owned) by demon spirits

"Heavenly Father, I praise You that although Satan may attempt to attack and afflict me, a demon spirit will never be able to own me. I thank You that the Word of God states that I have been bought by Jesus Christ, I am owned by Jesus Christ, I am sealed by Jesus Christ, and I am kept by Jesus Christ. I praise You that all of the powers of darkness who have invaded my life are subject to my will and they are merely trespassers and squatters who have no legal right to remain and must leave." *See* 1 Cor. 7:23, Rom. 8:9, 1 Cor. 6:19-20, Eph. 4:30, John 10:28, Luke 10:20, and Matt. 16:19.

Prayer to test presence of demon spirits

"Heavenly Father, I take my spiritual authority, which I have as I am 'seated in Christ' at Your right hand, and I bind the demon spirits that may be present, and I command them to manifest and reveal their presence." *See* Eph. 2:6, Mark 5:1-10, Luke 10:20, and Matt. 16:19.

CHAPTER 11 – ACTIVITIES OF DEMONS

Prayer against sexual temptation before marriage

"Heavenly Father, I praise You that You created me as a sexual being. Yet, I do not want the powers of darkness to exploit my God-given sexual desires and enslave me to evil desires. I pray for sexual purity in my life. I pray that I would not dwell on immoral thoughts and sexual fantasies.

I present my body to You as a living and holy sacrifice. Help me to avoid sexual temptation and not watch sexual scenes on the internet or in movies. Give me strength to cut off all relationships in my life that tempt me to have sex before marriage. I pray that You will bring someone into my life so I can express my sexuality (after marriage) in a way that honors You." *See* 2 Tim. 2:22, Matt. 15:19, Acts 15:20, Ps. 101:3, and 1 Cor. 6:9.

Prayer against sexual temptation after marriage

"Heavenly Father, I thank You for my spouse. I commit my sexual relationship with my spouse to You. I pray that my sex life would be everything that You designed it to be. I pray that You give me grace to understand that my spouse's level of desire for sex may be different than mine. Help me not to be sexually selfish toward my spouse. I pray for sexual purity in my life. I pray against the temptation of having sex with someone who is not my spouse. I pray that I would not dwell on immoral thoughts and sexual fantasies. I present my body to You as a living and holy sacrifice. Help me to avoid sexual temptation and not watch sexual scenes on the internet or in movies. I pray that I would be satisfied and have a deep and meaningful sex life with my spouse." *See* 1 Cor. 7:5, 2 Tim. 2:22, Ps. 101:3, and Heb. 13:4.

Prayer against giving up emotionally on your spouse

"Heavenly Father, my spouse has hurt me emotionally. I feel very angry and bitter. I am at a point where I have no desire to continue in this relationship. I am emotionally exhausted. I confess that I do not have any positive feelings for my spouse. Right now, I give to You all of my negative feelings. I repent of bitterness, anger, and my desire to get out of this marriage. I ask that You intervene and heal my marriage. I pray that You would help me love my spouse in the same way that You love me, even with all of my faults. I pray against the temptation of giving up emotionally on my spouse." *See* Eph. 4:31 and Heb. 12:15.

Prayer against romantic fantasies

"Heavenly Father, I feel there is an emotional hole in my heart. I confess that I am drawn to romantic books and fantasies about having a new relationship. I pray against the powers of darkness deceiving me to live in a fantasy world. I know these fantasies are built on unrealistic expectations. I pray that You would heal my marriage. I pray that I would find romance and satisfaction with my spouse." *See* 2 Cor. 10:5, Matt. 5:28, and Matt. 19:9.

Prayer against jealousy and self-ambition

"Heavenly Father, I pray that You would guard my heart against jealousy and self-ambition. I clothe myself with humility. I pray that the work that I do in my home, at my job, and in ministry, would be for Your glory and not for my self-promotion. Guard my heart from being jealous of another person's talents, money, position, or ministry." *See* Jam. 3:14-15, Col. 3:12, Heb. 13:5, 1 John 2:16, and Jam. 4:10.

Prayer for wisdom in deciding the type of music to enjoy

"Heavenly Father, I pray that You would be glorified in the type of music that I listen to. I pray that the Holy Spirit would convict me and prick my conscience if a particular song does not honor You. Please take my desire away for music that provokes vain imagination, violence, or worldliness." *See* Ezek. 28:13, 1 John 2:15-16, 1 John 4:5, 1 Sam. 16:23, and Jam. 1:5.

Prayer to remove demonic presence in home

"Heavenly Father, I have sensed an unusual manifestation in my home. You know if this manifestation is just my vivid imagination, or a demon spirit seeking to disturb me and create fear and anxiety. I reject all fear and anxiety. I pray that You would give me wisdom and sound judgment to determine the source of this apparent manifestation. If this manifestation was caused by a demon spirit, I take my spiritual authority, which I have as I am 'seated in Christ' at Your right hand, and I bind all the demon spirits that are present in my home. I command them to leave immediately and go to the pit. I pray that You would send the holy angels to surround my home and wage war against the powers of darkness. I pray that I would experience the peace which only the Holy Spirit can give me." *See* Lev. 19:31, 1 Sam. 28:7-12, Eph. 2:6, and Matt. 16:19.

CHAPTER 12 – SINS OF PAST GENERATIONS

Prayer to break demonic stronghold over a child

"Heavenly Father, I commit my children to You. I pray that one day they will accept Your offer of a pardon and completely serve You. Until that day, I stand in the gap for my children. I take my spiritual authority, which I have as I am 'seated in Christ' at Your right hand, and I break all demonic strongholds in my children. I bind all demon spirits who are seeking to attack or harm any of my children. I command that these demon spirits be sent to the pit." *See* Mark 7:25-26, Mark 9:17-21, Luke 10:17-19, Eph. 2:6, and Matt. 16:19.

Prayer to break all demonic strongholds regardless of origin

"Heavenly Father, I take my spiritual authority, which I have as I am 'seated in Christ' at Your right hand, and I bind the demon spirits who have any strongholds in my life *regardless of how such bondage originated*. I thank You that my relationship with Satan has been severed because of the blood of Christ. I command all demon spirits to leave me and go to the pit." *See* Exod. 20:4-5, Eph. 2:6, Matt. 16:19, Jer. 32:17-18, John 9:2-3, Ezek. 18:20, Rom. 5:9, Heb. 4:13, and Luke 10:17-19.

SPIRITUAL
WARFARE

Example Prayers for Removing Demonic Strongholds

PRE-COUNSELING PREPARATION

1. Ask God to reveal any unrepented sin in your life.

"Heavenly Father, I pray that You would put Your searchlight on my heart and bring to my mind sins that I have committed in the past but have never repented of. I want to make sure that all doors that I have opened to the powers of darkness through my unrepented sin are now closed." *See* Ps. 139:23.

2. Surrender all areas in your life to the Holy Spirit and be filled.

"Heavenly Father, I have repented of all my known past sins. I have closed the doors to the powers of darkness in my life. I now surrender every area in my life (every room in my house) to the Holy Spirit.

Specifically, I yield the area of **[Specifically Name Each Area]** to the Holy Spirit. I give You permission to clean and remodel each room. I pray and claim in faith that I would be filled with the Holy Spirit." *See* Eph. 5:18 and 2 Cor. 5:7.

Note – Refer to Appendix: "Areas to Surrender to the Holy Spirit."

3. Ask God for protection.

"Heavenly Father, I praise You that You have assigned holy angels to guard me in all my ways. I praise You that the holy angels are powerful. I pray that the holy angels would protect me against the demon spirits who are tempting me, deceiving me, and seeking to obtain a stronghold in my life. I pray that You would have the holy angels execute Your fierce wrath and judgment against the demon spirits and destroy them." *See* Ps. 91:11, 2 Kings 6:15-17, Dan. 10:12-13, Rev. 12:7, 2 Thess. 3:3, and Matt. 26:53.

4. Put on each piece of the Armor of God.

Belt of Truth

"Heavenly Father, I put on the Belt of Truth. I pray that You would reveal any misunderstanding that I have in doctrine or practice regarding the Word of God. Please show me the lies that I have believed about myself, other people, You, and Satan. Please reveal all lies and deception in my life." *See* Eph. 6:14 and 2 Tim. 4:3.

Breastplate of Righteousness

"Heavenly Father, I put on the Breastplate of Righteousness. I thank You that I have been forgiven of all my past, present, and future sins. I thank You that there is no condemnation for those who have accepted Your offer of a pardon. I thank You that when You look upon me, You see that I am clothed with the very righteousness of Jesus Christ. I also pray that I would turn away from temptation and live in a righteous manner before You today." *See* Rom. 5:17, Rom. 10:9-10, Rom. 8:1, Titus 2:11-12, and 1 John 3:7-8.

Gospel Shoes

"Heavenly Father, I put on the Gospel Shoes. I pray that You would help me to be prepared to share the Gospel with anyone that You bring across my path today. I pray that You would grant me boldness and confidence. I thank You that the Holy Spirit can also give me peace when turmoil and trials come into my life. I claim the peace of God in my life." *See* Eph. 6:15, John 16:33, 1 Pet. 3:15, and Eph. 6:19.

Shield of Faith

"Heavenly Father, I take up the Shield of Faith. I thank You that I can trust in the promises that You have made to me in the Word of God. I praise You that You are always with me and will never desert me. I praise You that You want to help me and give me wisdom. I reject all thoughts that tempt me to doubt Your Word, Your goodness, Your existence, Your power, and Your great love for me. I praise You that

You are trustworthy, faithful, and always keep Your promises." *See* Eph. 6:16, Rom. 10:17, Gen. 28:15, Isa. 41;10, Gen. 3:1-5, Jam. 1:5, and Heb. 13:5.

Helmet of Salvation

"Heavenly Father, I take up the Helmet of Salvation. I thank You that I have accepted your offer of a pardon. I thank You that I am part of the Kingdom of God. I praise You that I have the assurance of salvation and that my name has been written in the Book of Life." *See* Eph. 6:17 and 1 John 5:13.

Sword of the Spirit

"Heavenly Father, I take up the Sword of the Spirit, which is the Word of God. I praise You that Your Word is powerful. I pray that Your Word would be as a sword (dagger) against the powers of darkness to overcome temptation in my life." *See* Eph. 6:17, Luke 4:9-12, and Ps. 119:11.

5. Pray that God would reveal the open doors to the person.

"Heavenly Father, I pray that You would reveal to **[Name of Person]** all doors that have been opened to the powers of darkness through their unrepented sin or deception. I pray that You would put Your searchlight on their heart and bring to their mind sins they have committed in the past but have never repented of. I pray that **[Name of Person]** would have the grace to repent of these sins. I also pray that **[Name of Person]** would reject the lies about themselves, others, You, and Satan." *See* Ps. 139:23 and 2 Tim. 2:26.

6. Pray that God would send holy angels to weaken the demon spirits.

"Heavenly Father, I pray that You would send the holy angels to **[Name of Person].** I pray that the holy angels would wage war against the powers of darkness. I pray that You would weaken the grip that the powers of darkness have on **[Name of Person]**. I pray that You would send Your terror ahead of me and throw into confusion all of the powers of darkness. I pray that the powers of darkness would tremble and be in anguish because of Your great name and power. Take note that these demon spirits have risen up against You. I pray that you would overthrow them and send forth your burning anger to consume and destroy them." *See* Exod. 15:7, Exod. 23:27, Deut. 2:25, Ps. 91:11, and Rev. 12:7.

DIRECT CONFRONTATION

Preliminary prayer requests

1. Pray for wisdom and discernment.

"Heavenly Father, we pray for wisdom and discernment. We praise You that You love **[Name of Person]**. We ask that You extend Your mercy and grace. We pray that You would guide us as we counsel **[Name of Person]** and seek to determine if the powers of darkness have been able to develop a stronghold in their life." *See* Jam. 1:5, 1 Cor. 12:10, and 2 Tim. 2:26.

2. Pray for protection against the powers of darkness.

"Heavenly Father, we pray for protection against the powers of darkness. We pray that You would protect **[Name of Person]**, everyone present, and our families as we battle the powers of darkness. We ask that You protect everyone physically and spiritually. We thank You that You are with us. It is in Your name that we come against these powers. We pray that You would be as a shield to us. We thank You that Satan and his hosts have already been defeated when Jesus Christ died on the cross, shed His blood, paid the penalty for our sin, and arose from the dead. We pray that each person's guardian angels would be present. We pray that a multitude of holy angels would form a wall of fire around us. We ask that the holy angels with their flaming swords would stand between us and the demon spirits. We thank You that You are almighty, all powerful, and there is none who can deliver out of Your hand." *See* Ps. 91:11, 2 Kings 6:15-17, Dan. 10:12-13, Rev. 12:7, Matt. 10:19, Col. 1:13, Rev. 12:11, 2 Thess. 3:3, Isa. 43:13, 2 Chron. 14:11, and Matt. 26:53.

3. Pray for holy angels to surround geographical area.

"Heavenly Father, thank You for the holy angels. We thank You that they continually wage war against the powers of darkness. We know that Your Word describes in the Book of Daniel the spiritual battles between holy angels and the demons over geographical areas such as Greece and Persia. We know that this is also true where we live. We ask that You send a multitude of the holy angels to surround the geographical area of **[Name of Area]**. We pray that You would create a buffer zone around us to prevent Satan and his hosts from interfering as we seek to remove any demonic strongholds in **[Name of Person]**." *See* Ps. 91:11, 2 Kings 6:15-17, Dan. 10:12-13, and 2 Thess. 3:3.

Preliminary commands to the demon spirits

1. Command demon spirits not to speak unless you ask a question.

   "Heavenly Father, I take my spiritual authority, which I have as I am 'seated in Christ' at Your right hand, and I command that all demon spirits that may be in **[Name of Person]** are not to speak unless I ask a question. I command the demon spirits not to interrupt, distract, or interfere in any way as we seek to remove them." *See* Eph. 2:6, Mark 1:25, Luke 10:19-20, Mark 1:34, and Matt. 16:19.

2. Command demon spirits not to hurt the person when they leave.

   "Heavenly Father, I take my spiritual authority, which I have as I am 'seated in Christ' at Your right hand, and I command that all demon spirits that may be present are not to hurt or harm **[Name of Person]** in any way. I pray that You would have the holy angels enforce this command and punish the demon spirits if they disobey." *See* Luke 4:35, Luke 10:19-20, Matt. 16:19, and Eph. 2:6.

3. Command demon spirits to go to the pit when they leave.

"Heavenly Father, I take my spiritual authority, which I have as I am 'seated in Christ' at Your right hand, and I command that all demon spirits present are to go straight to the pit when they leave. I pray that these demon spirits would be delivered into Your hands and You would remove them from the face of the earth. I pray that You would have the holy angels escort the demons to the pit and confine them there until their final judgment. I pray that You would not let one of them escape." *See* Acts 16:16-18, Eph. 2:6, Matt. 16:19, and Deut. 7:24.

KEY STEPS TO FREEDOM

1. Confirm that the person has accepted God's offer of a pardon.

"God, I admit that I have sinned. I believe the penalty of my sin is eternal punishment. I believe that Your son Jesus Christ died on a cross, shed His blood to pay the penalty for my sin, and arose from the dead. I commit my life to Jesus Christ. I submit to Jesus Christ as the absolute boss and authority of my life. I repent of my sin. I confess Jesus Christ as my Lord. I accept Your offer of a pardon by faith." *See* Rom.

3:23, Rom. 6:23, John 3:16, Rom. 10:9, Luke 13:5, and Eph. 2:8-9.

Note: Explain that prayer can be an expression of faith. Have the person pray this salvation prayer but explain they must sincerely mean it and exercise faith in God. Merely repeating a prayer will not save anyone.

2. Identify all open doors in the person's life.

"Heavenly Father, I pray that You would put Your searchlight on my heart and bring to my mind sins that I have committed in the past but have never repented of. I want to make sure that all doors that I have opened to the powers of darkness through my unrepented sin are now closed." *See* Ps. 139:23.

Note: Have the person pray this prayer. As the Holy Spirit brings to the person's mind sins committed in the past, those sins must be repented of.

3. Command the demon spirits to reveal their presence.

"Heavenly Father, I take my spiritual authority which I have as I am 'seated in Christ' at Your right hand, and I bind the demon spirits that may be present in **[Name of Person]** and I command them to manifest and reveal their presence." *See* Eph. 4:27, Eph. 2:6, Mark 5:1-10, Luke 10:20-21, and Matt. 16:19.

4. Command the demon spirits to leave the person.

"Heavenly Father, I take my spiritual authority which I have as I am 'seated in Christ' at Your right hand, and I bind the demon spirits who have created a spiritual stronghold in the area of **[Name Area]** and I command them to leave and go to the pit." *See* Acts 16:16-18, Eph. 2:6, and Matt. 16:19.

5. Ask that the Holy Spirit would fill the spiritual vacuum after the demon spirits depart.

"Heavenly Father, I have repented of all known past sins. I have closed the doors to the powers of darkness in my life. I now surrender every area in my life (every room in my house) to the Holy Spirit. Specifically, I yield the area of **[Name Area]** to the Holy Spirit. I give You permission to begin cleaning and remodeling this room. I pray and claim in faith that I would be filled with the Holy Spirit." *See* Eph. 5:18 and 2 Cor. 5:7.

Note - Have the person pray this prayer.

SPIRITUAL WARFARE

Removing Demonic Stronghold Checklist

PRE-COUNSELING PREPARATION

1. Ask God to reveal any unrepented sin in your life.

2. Surrender all areas in your life to the Holy Spirit and claim His fullness.

3. Ask God for protection.

4. Put on each piece of the Armor of God.

5. Pray that God would reveal the open doors to the person.

6. Pray that God would send the holy angels to weaken the demon spirits.

DIRECT CONFRONTATION
Preliminary prayer requests

1. Pray for wisdom and discernment.

2. Pray for protection against the powers of darkness.

3. Pray that God would have the holy angels surround the geographical area.

Preliminary commands to the demon spirits

1. Command the demon spirits not to speak unless you ask a question.

2. Command the demon spirits not to hurt the person when they leave.

3. Command the demon spirits to go to the pit when they leave.

KEY STEPS TO FREEDOM

1. Confirm that the person has accepted God's offer of a pardon.

2. Identify all open doors in the person's life.

3. Command the demon spirits to manifest and reveal their presence.

4. Command the demon spirits to leave the person.

5. Ask that the Holy Spirit would fill the spiritual vacuum after the demon departs.

MAINTAINING YOUR FREEDOM

1. Daily prayer.

2. Read the Word of God.

3. Fellowship with other believers.

4. Share the Gospel.

WARNINGS

1. Do not blame everything on demon spirits.

2. All diseases and illnesses are not caused by demon spirits.

3. Mental challenges are not always demonic.

4. Unrepented sin does not mean a person has a demon spirit.

5. Rebuking of demon spirits should never be spectacularized.

6. Test all teachings on spiritual warfare by the Word of God.

SPIRITUAL
WARFARE

Verses for Defeating Fear and Anxiety

"When I am afraid, I will put my trust in You" (Ps. 56:3).

"Do not fear, for I am with you; Do not anxiously look about you, for I am your God. I will strengthen you, surely I will help you, Surely I will uphold you with My righteous right hand" (Isa. 41:10).

"Do not be afraid of sudden fear Nor the onslaught of the wicked when it comes; For the LORD will be your confidence and will keep your foot from being caught" (Prov. 3:25-26).

"Do not fear, for I have redeemed you; I have called you by name; you are Mine!" (Isa. 43:1).

"I sought the LORD, and He answered me, and delivered me from all my fears" (Ps. 34:4).

"The fear of man brings a snare, But he who trusts in the LORD will be exalted" Prov. 29:25).

"I will go before you and make the rough places smooth" (Isa. 45:2).

"Trust in the LORD with all your heart And do not lean on your own understanding. In all your ways acknowledge Him, And He will make your paths straight" (Prov. 3:5-6).

"You shall not dread them, for the LORD your God is in your midst, a great and awesome God" (Deut. 7:21).

"I, even I, am He who comforts you. Who are you that you are afraid of man who dies and the son of man who is made like grass, That you have forgotten the LORD your Maker, Who stretched out the heavens and laid the foundations of the earth, That you fear continually all day long because of the fury of the oppressor…?" (Isa. 51:12-13).

"Do not fear those who kill the body but are unable to kill the soul; but rather fear Him who is able to destroy both soul and body in hell" (Matt. 10:28).

"So do not worry about tomorrow; for tomorrow will care for itself. Each day has enough trouble of its own" (Matt. 6:34).

"The LORD said to Moses, 'Is the LORD's power limited? Now you shall see whether My word will come true for you or not'" (Num. 11:23).

"Those who know Your name will put their trust in You, For You, O LORD, have not forsaken those who seek You" (Ps. 9:10)

"The LORD has established His throne in the heavens, and His sovereignty rules over all" (Ps. 103:19).

"The angel of the LORD encamps around those who fear Him, And rescues them" (Ps. 34:7).

"You will not be afraid of the terror by night, Or of the arrow that flies by day" (Ps. 91:5).

"He will give His angels charge concerning you, To guard you in all your ways" (Ps. 91:11).

"The steadfast of mind You will keep in perfect peace, Because he trusts in You" (Isa. 26:3).

"Peace I leave with you; My peace I give to you; not as the world gives do I give to you. Do not let your heart be troubled, nor let it be fearful" (John 14:27).

"Cast your burden upon the LORD, and He will sustain you; He will never allow the righteous to be shaken" (Ps. 55:22).

"In the day of my trouble I shall call upon You, For You will answer me" (Ps. 86:7).

"The LORD said to him, 'Who has made man's mouth? Or who makes him mute or deaf, or seeing or blind? Is it not I, the LORD? Now then go, and I, even I, will be with your mouth, and teach you what you are to say'" (Exod. 4:11-12).

"Behold, I am with you and will keep you wherever you go, and will bring you back to this land; for I will not leave you until I have done what I have promised you" (Gen. 28:15).

"The LORD will fight for you while you keep silent" (Exod. 14:14).

"The eyes of the LORD move to and fro throughout the earth that He may strongly support those whose heart is completely His" (2 Chron. 16:9).

"He who touches you, touches the apple of His eye" (Zech. 2:8).

"The LORD is with me like a dread champion; therefore my persecutors will stumble and not prevail" (Jer. 20:11).

"Though a host encamp against me, My heart will not fear; Though war arise against me, In spite of this I shall be confident" (Ps. 27:3).

"The very hairs of your head are all numbered" (Matt. 10:30).

"But as for me, I would seek God, And I would place my cause before God; Who does great and unsearchable things, Wonders without number" (Job 5:8-9).

"'I know the plans that I have for you,' declares the LORD, 'plans for welfare and not for calamity to give you a future and a hope. Then you will call upon Me and come and pray to Me, and I will listen to you. You will seek Me and find Me when you search for Me with all your heart'" (Jer. 29:11-13).

"Ah Lord God! Behold, You have made the heavens and the earth by Your great power and by Your outstretched arm! Nothing is too difficult for You" (Jer. 32:17).

"The LORD is good, A stronghold in the day of trouble, And He knows those who take refuge in Him" (Nahum 1:7).

"When they deliver you up, do not worry about how or what you are to say; for it will be given you in that hour what you are to say. For it is not you who speak, but it is the Spirit of your Father who speaks in you" (Mat 10:19-20).

"It will lead to an opportunity for your testimony. So make up you minds not to prepare beforehand to defend yourselves; for I will give you utterance and wisdom which none of your opponents will be able to resist or refute" (Luke 21:13-15).

"Be on guard, so that your hearts will not be weighted down with dissipation and drunkenness and the worries of life, and that day will not come on you suddenly like a trap; for it will come upon all those who dwell on the face of all the earth" (Luke 21:34-35).

"I know that You can do all things, And that no purpose of Yours can be thwarted" (Job 42:2).

"Your lovingkindness, O LORD, extends to the heavens, Your faithfulness reaches to the skies" (Ps. 36:5).

SPIRITUAL
WARFARE

Verses for Destruction of Demonic Strongholds and Protection

"This day I will begin to put the dread and fear of you upon the peoples everywhere under the heavens, who, when they hear the report of you, will tremble and be in anguish because of you" (Deut. 2:25).

"He will deliver their kings into your hand so that you will make their name perish from under heaven; no man will be able to stand before you until you have destroyed them" (Deut. 7:24).

"You shall consume all the peoples whom the LORD your God will deliver to you; your eye shall not pity them" (Deut. 7:16).

"I will send My terror ahead of you, and throw into confusion all the people among whom you come, and I will make all your enemies turn their backs to you" (Exod. 23:27).

"You shall not dread them, for the LORD your God is in your midst, a great and awesome God" (Deut. 7:21).

"Even from eternity I am He, And there is none who can deliver out of My hand; I act and who can reverse it?" (Isa. 43:13).

"In the greatness of Your excellence You overthrow those who rise up against You; You send forth Your burning anger, and it consumes them as chaff" (Exod. 15:7).

"Only do not rebel against the LORD; and do not fear the people of the land, for they will be our prey. Their protection has been removed from them, and the LORD is with us; do not fear them" (Num. 14:9).

"Behold, I have given you authority to tread on serpents and scorpions, and over all the power of the enemy, and nothing will injure you" (Luke 10:19).

"Do not rejoice in this, that the spirits are subject to you, but rejoice that your names are recorded in heaven" (Luke 10:20).

"LORD, there is no one besides You to help in the battle between the powerful and those who have no strength; so help us, O LORD our God, for we trust in You, and in Your name have come against this multitude. O LORD, You are our God; let not man prevail against You" (2 Chron. 14:11).

"The eyes of the LORD move to and fro throughout the earth that He may strongly support those whose heart is completely His" (2 Chron. 16:9).

"The Lord is with me like a dread champion; Therefore my persecutors will stumble and not prevail" (Jer. 20:11).

"Contend, O LORD, with those who contend with me; Fight against those who fight against me" (Ps. 35:1).

"Oh give us help against the adversary, for deliverance by man is vain. Through God we shall do valiantly, and it is He who will tread down our adversaries" (Ps. 108:12-13).

"In your lovingkindness, cut off my enemies And destroy all those who afflict my soul, for I am Your servant" (Ps. 143:12).

"I will contend with the one who contends with you" (Isa. 49:25).

"'They will fight against you, but they will not overcome you, for I am with you to deliver you,' declares the LORD" (Jer. 1:19).

"'I,' declares the LORD, 'will be a wall of fire around her, and I will be the glory in her midst'" (Zech. 2:5).

"He who touches you, touches the apple of His eye" (Zech 2:8).

"I will give you the keys of the kingdom of heaven; and whatever you bind on earth shall have been bound in heaven, and whatever you loose on earth shall have been loosed in heaven" (Matt. 16:19).

"He will give His angels charge concerning you, to guard you in all your ways" (Ps. 91:11).

"The chariots of God are myriads, thousands upon thousands" (Ps. 68:17).

"See that you do not despise one of these little ones, for I say to you that their angels in heaven continually see the face of My Father who is in heaven" (Matt. 18:10).

"Do you think that I cannot appeal to My Father, and He will at once put at My disposal more than twelve legions of angels?" (Matt. 26:53).

"If I cast out demons by the finger of God, then the kingdom of God has come upon you. When a strong man, fully armed, guards his own house, his possessions are undisturbed. But when someone stronger than he attacks him and overpowers him, he takes away from him all his armor on which he had relied and distributes his plunder" (Luke 11:20-22).

"I do not ask You to take them out of the world, but to keep them from the evil one" (John 17:15).

"How is it you were not afraid to stretch out your hand to destroy the LORD's anointed?" (2 Sam. 1:14).

Sinventory

"A SIN PRAYER GUIDE FOR THE BELIEVER"

FORWARD

Revival! Thousands of revival meetings are held every year in the United States. However, only a very few churches experience true revival. Unfortunately, revival services are often only a series of poorly attended meetings.

God desires to bring revival to the church. Yet, believers are often not willing to receive revival on God's terms. Revival only comes when believers, in response to the conviction of the Holy Spirit, humble themselves and turn to God through repentance of sin. Without genuine repentance there will be no revival. Repentance prepares the heart for the fullness of the Holy Spirit and the movement of God in a church. Unrepented sin is what prevents revival in many churches.

The Sinventory is a prayer guide for the believer. A person who has not experienced salvation will not find peace with God by merely refraining from certain sins or attempting to live a holy life. It is only by receiving forgiveness of sin through the death, burial, and resurrection of Jesus Christ that a person inherits eternal life. Furthermore, a person who has received Jesus Christ as his Lord and Savior never needs to fear the wrath of God because the penalty of his sin has been paid by Jesus Christ through the shedding of His blood on the cross.

After salvation, the Holy Spirit will convict the believer when he or she sins. If the believer ignores the conviction of the Holy Spirit and fails to repent, sin will begin to gain power over the believer. The believer has an eternal relationship with God that can never be severed. However, sin can block the believer's fellowship with God. Satan can also use unrepented sin to obtain a foothold in the believer's life to create a spiritual bondage.

Often the believer does not take enough time from his busy schedule to read and meditate on the Word of God and allow the Holy Spirit to point out sin in his life. At other times, the Holy Spirit will convict the believer of sin, but he or she fails to promptly repent and soon forgets that they sinned against God.

The Sinventory quotes key portions of Scripture and provides questions for the believer to consider and reflect upon. During this process, the Holy Spirit will point out unrepented sins in the believer's life. These sins may be hindering the believer from experiencing personal revival and growing spiritually. However, the Sinventory should not be used as a legalistic guide to find sin. The believer should only repent of sin based on the conviction of the Holy Spirit.

Example prayer for God to reveal unrepented sin:

"Heavenly Father, I pray that You would put Your searchlight on my heart and bring to my mind sins that I have committed in the past but have never repented of. I want to make sure that all doors in my life that I have opened to the powers of darkness are closed."

Example prayer to repent of sin:

"Heavenly Father, I repent of _____. I turn from this sin. I thank you for the forgiveness that I have because Jesus Christ shed His blood on the cross. Please cleanse me from this sin. I now shut the door in my life to the powers of darkness that I previously opened by this unrepented sin."

"If we confess our sins, He is faithful and righteous to forgive us our sins and to cleanse us from all unrighteousness" (1 John 1:9).

LYING

"Do not lie to one another, since you laid aside the old self with its evil practices" (Col. 3:9).

Have you lied? Have you been untruthful by withholding information or twisting the truth? Have you lied at your job? Have you lied to your spouse? Have you lied on your income taxes? Have you slandered someone? Have you listened to someone slander another person when you could have avoided the situation?

COMPLAINING

"Do all things without grumbling or disputing" (Phil. 2:14).

Have you grumbled or complained? Have you complained to God? Have you complained about the way God made you? Have you complained to God that He has not given you the money you think you need? Have you complained about your church? Have you grumbled about the working conditions at your job or not having a job? Have you nagged and complained to your spouse? Have you complained to others about your spouse?

GOSSIP

"I am afraid that perhaps when I come I may find you to be not what I wish and may be found by you to be not what you wish; that perhaps there will be strife, jealousy, angry tempers, disputes, slanders, gossip, arrogance, disturbances" (2 Cor. 12:20).

Have you gossiped? Have you gossiped about your pastor? Have you gossiped about a co-worker or your boss? Have you said something that was true about another person but was not edifying or was said in anger, envy, or bitterness? Have you posted on social media unkind remarks about someone? Have you ever gossiped about celebrities, politicians, or people you do not know personally?

SELFISHNESS

"Do nothing from selfishness or empty conceit, but with humility of mind regard one another as more important than yourselves" (Phil. 2:3).

Have you been selfish? Have you been selfish with your material possessions? Have you been selfish with your time? Have you been sexually selfish with your spouse?

LUST FOR POWER

"An argument started among them as to which of them might be the greatest. But Jesus, knowing what they were thinking in their heart, took a child and stood him by His side, and said to them, 'Whoever receives this child in My name receives Me, and whoever receives Me receives Him who sent Me; for the one who is least among all of you, this is the one who is great'" (Luke 9:46-48).

Have you desired to be great in the world's eyes? Have you lusted for power over people? Do you fantasize about being a man or woman of great wealth? Is it your ambition to be a famous evangelist, pastor, or minister regardless of God's will for your life? Have you fantasized about being a great businessman, rock star, actor, politician, or world leader and having people idolize you?

STUBBORNNESS

"Because of your stubbornness and unrepentant heart you are storing up wrath for yourself in the day of wrath and revelation of the righteous judgment of God" (Rom. 2:5).

Have you been stubborn? Have you been stubborn in accepting other people's advice? Have you been stubborn with your spouse in refusing to listen to her or his suggestions? Do you always want to be the decision maker? Do you have to have your way in the church as a condition of your support and cooperation? Have you been stubborn in not obeying God?

IMPATIENCE

"We urge you, brethren, admonish the unruly, encourage the fainthearted, help the weak, be patient with everyone" (1 Thess. 5:14).

Have you been impatient with people? Have you been impatient with your spouse or children? Have you been impatient with your co-workers? Have you been impatient with yourself? Have you been impatient with God?

ARGUMENTS

"The Lord's bond-servant must not be quarrelsome, but be kind to all, able to teach, patient when wronged" (2 Tim. 2:24).

Have you been argumentative or quarrelsome? Have you quarreled or bickered with your spouse, parents, or children? Do you provoke quarrels by making abrasive comments? Have you argued about Bible doctrine? Have you ever been argumentative at a church business meeting?

TEMPER

"A fool always loses his temper, But a wise man holds it back" (Prov. 29:11).

Have you lost your temper? Have you lost your temper with your spouse or children? Have you lost your temper while at your job, school, church, or a social setting? Have you lost your temper with a stranger, *i.e.*, over the phone, when you feel you are not getting the response you desire?

BITTERNESS

"Let all bitterness and wrath and anger and clamor and slander be put away from you, along with all malice" (Eph. 4:31).

Have you been bitter toward anyone? Have you been bitter at God? Have you been bitter against a former employer? Have you been bitter at your spouse? Are you bitter because you believe someone has let you down by not meeting your expectations?

UNFORGIVENESS

"If you forgive others for their transgressions, your heavenly Father will also forgive you. But if you do

not forgive others, then your Father will not forgive your transgressions" (Matt. 6:14-15).

Is there anyone that you hold a grudge against? Is there anyone, including a business partner, ex-spouse, pastor, or relative, who has hurt you in the past that you have not forgiven? Have you forgiven yourself of sins you have sincerely repented of?

REVENGE

"Never take your own revenge, beloved, but leave room for the wrath of God, for it is written, 'Vengeance is Mine, I will repay,' says the Lord. But if your enemy is hungry, feed him, and if he is thirsty, give him a drink; for in so doing you will heap burning coals upon his head'" (Rom. 12:19-20).

Have you taken revenge against someone? Do you have vengeful thoughts in your heart? Do you wish you could kill or harm someone? Do you have thoughts of destroying someone financially or their business? Do you think about getting even with people who have wronged you in the past?

HATE

"We also once were foolish ourselves, disobedient, deceived, enslaved to various lusts and pleasures, spending our life in malice and envy, hateful, hating one another" (Titus 3:3).

Have you hated anyone? Do you hate your boss or teachers? Do you hate your parents or in-laws? If you are divorced, do you hate your former spouse? Do you hate your government leaders?

PROFANITY

"Let no unwholesome word proceed from your mouth, but only such a word is good for edification according to the need of the moment, so that it may give grace to those who hear" (Eph. 4:29).

Have you used unwholesome language? Do you swear? Have you used words to verbally abuse or demean another person? Have you used God's name in vain?

IMMORAL JOKES

"There must be no filthiness and silly talk, or coarse jesting, which are not fitting, but rather giving of thanks" (Eph. 5:4).

Have you told filthy or immoral jokes? Have you listened to an immoral joke when you could have avoided the situation?

STEALING

"You shall not steal" (Exod. 20:15).

Have you stolen anything? Have you shoplifted? Have you stolen anything from your employer? Have you exaggerated income tax deductions? Have you claimed business deductions for things that were not business related? Have you engaged in personal activities on your employer's time? Have you used your employer's equipment or supplies for personal matters without permission?

DOUBT

"He must ask in faith without any doubting, for the one who doubts is like the surf of the sea, driven and tossed by the wind" (Jam. 1:6).

Have you doubted the Word of God? Do you doubt that God loves you? Do you doubt that God exists? Do you doubt that God is all powerful? Do you doubt that God can provide your physical needs? Do you doubt that God can work for His glory in the difficult circumstances of your life?

UNBELIEF

"You will say then, 'Branches were broken off so that I might be grafted in.' Quite right, they were broken off for their unbelief, but you stand by your faith. Do not be conceited, but fear; for if God did not spare the natural branches, He will not spare you, either" (Rom. 11:19-21).

Have you chosen to not believe certain portions of the Word of God? Have you rationalized certain passages of Scripture to justify a moral failure in your life?

LACK OF THANKSGIVING

"Devote yourselves to prayer, keeping alert in it with an attitude of thanksgiving" (Col. 4:2).

Have you failed to maintain an attitude of praise and thanksgiving? Have you failed to thank God for the good things that He has brought into your life? Do you give thanks in all things even for the difficult circumstances in your life? Have you neglected personal praise and worship?

LACK OF PRAYER

"Pray without ceasing" (1 Thess. 5:17).

Have you neglected prayer? Have you failed to make prayer a priority in your life? Have you made significant decisions in your life without consulting God?

INEFFECTIVE PRAYER

"When you are praying, do not use meaningless repetition, as the Gentiles do, for they suppose that they will be heard for their many words" (Matt. 6:7).

Do you pray out of a sense of obligation rather than a desire to develop a personal relationship with God? Have you used meaningless repetition when addressing God? If you pray before your meals, has it become a mere habit? Do you pray for material blessings when you know there is unrepented sin in your life?

LACK OF BIBLE STUDY

"Be diligent to present yourself approved to God as a workman who does not need to be ashamed, accurately handling the word of truth" (2 Tim. 2:15).

Have you neglected to read and study the Bible? Do you feel you know everything about the Bible? Do you have an unteachable heart? Are you seeking God's guidance when you read God's Word?

LACK OF FELLOWSHIP

"Not forsaking our own assembling together, as is the habit of some, but encouraging one another, and all the more, as you see the day drawing near" (Heb. 10:25).

Have you neglected fellowship with other believers? Do you feel you do not need fellowship with other believers to grow spiritually? Have you failed to fellowship with others to meet their spiritual needs? Have you excused yourself from attending a local church because you have not found the "perfect church" or believe that you do not need "organized religion?"

RELATIONSHIP TO GOD

"Behold, I stand at the door and knock; if anyone hears My voice and opens the door, I will come into him, and will dine with him, and he with Me" (Rev. 3:20).

Have you substituted going to church for a personal relationship with God? Have you confused religious busyness with personally knowing God? Do you find yourself going through religious motions without your heart really being involved?

TITHES AND OFFERINGS

"Woe to you, scribes and Pharisees, hypocrites! For you tithe mint and dill and cummin, and have neglected the weightier provisions of the law: justice and mercy and faithfulness; but these are the things you should have done without neglecting the others" *(Matt. 23:23).*

Have you neglected to give of your financial resources to God's work? Have you ever prayed and sincerely asked God to show you how much you should give to your church and to other ministries? Have you ever given an offering grudgingly? Have you ever given with selfish motives?

GREED

"Immorality or any impurity or greed must not even be named among you, as is proper among saints" *(Eph. 5:3).*

Have you been greedy? Have you failed to meet the physical needs of others? Do you resent churches or charities asking for donations? Have you hoarded money? Have you put your faith in your savings account or investments rather than trusting God for your future needs?

LACK OF DISCIPLINE

"Even though I am absent in body, nevertheless I am with you in spirit, rejoicing to see your good discipline and the stability of your faith in Christ" (Col. 2:5).

Do you lack discipline in spending money? Have you purchased items you could not afford? Have you lacked discipline in physical exercise? Have you failed to treat your body as the temple of the Holy Spirit? Do your habits harm your body? Have you failed to give your body the rest it needs?

EATING HABITS

"Many walk, of whom I often told you, and now tell you even weeping, that they are enemies of the cross of Christ, whose end is destruction, whose god is their appetite, and whose glory is in their shame, who set their minds on earthly things" (Phil. 3:18-19).

Is your god your appetite? Do you overeat when you are depressed or discouraged? Have you listened to the Holy Spirit in deciding the types and amounts of food you should eat? Are you overweight or underweight because of poor eating habits?

ALCOHOL

"Do you not know that the unrighteous shall not inherit the kingdom of God? Do not be deceived;

*neither fornicators, nor idolaters, nor adulterers, nor
effeminate, nor homosexuals, nor thieves, nor the
covetous, nor drunkards, nor revilers, nor swindlers,
will inherit the kingdom of God" (1 Cor. 6:9-10).*

Have you been drunk? Do you drink alcohol when you are
depressed or discouraged? Are you dependent on alcohol to
get through the day? Do you drink alcohol instead of turning to God to ease your emotional pain?

LAZINESS

*"Laziness casts into a deep sleep, and an idle man
will suffer hunger" (Prov. 19:15).*

Have you been lazy? Have you been lazy at your job? Have
you been lazy about Bible study? Have you been lazy about
cleaning and taking care of your home? Have you been lazy
about providing for the physical needs of your family?

JEALOUSY

*"You are still fleshly. For since there is jealousy and
strife among you, are you not fleshly, and are you
not walking like mere men?" (1 Cor. 3:3).*

Have you been jealous? Have you been jealous of someone because of her or his appearance, possessions, finances,
talents, or vocation? Have you been jealous of another
person's spiritual gift? Are you jealous of the ministry of
a famous minister or evangelist? Pastors, are you jealous
because of the large attendance at another church or the
size of the church building?

COVETOUSNESS

"You shall not covet your neighbor's house; you shall not covet your neighbor's wife or his male servant or his female servant or his ox or his donkey or anything that belongs to your neighbor" (Exod. 20:17).

Have you coveted someone's home, car, family, or lifestyle? Have you coveted the income someone else earns? Have you coveted material possessions? Do you wish you were married to someone else?

PRIDE

"When pride comes, then comes dishonor, But with the humble is wisdom" (Prov. 11:2).

Have you been prideful? Are you prideful of your education, occupation, or position in the church? Have you given God the glory for your accomplishments? Do you believe you are self-sufficient and really do not need any help from God? Are you prideful of your appearance? Are you proud that you give more money to the church than other people?

BRAGGING

"Love is patient, love is kind and is not jealous; love does not brag and is not arrogant" (1 Cor. 13:4).

Have you bragged? Have you bragged about how much of the Bible you know? Have you bragged about the material possessions you own? Do you always talk about yourself and your accomplishments?

DEPRESSION

> *"We know that God causes all things to work together for good to those who love God, to those who are called according to His purpose"* (Rom. 8:28).

Have you doubted that God can use your mistakes and the trials in your life for good? Have you given into attitudes of despair or depression? Is your life easily crushed by your circumstances because you have failed to trust in the Word of God?

LONELINESS

> *"I am convinced that neither death, nor life, nor angels, nor principalities, nor things present, nor things to come, nor powers, nor height, nor depth, nor any other created thing, will be able to separate us from the love of God, which is in Christ Jesus our Lord"* (Rom. 8:38-39).

Have you allowed loneliness to control your life instead of claiming the presence of Christ? Have you tried to fill a void in your life with human relationships as a substitute for a deep relationship with God?

REJECTION

"If anyone is in Christ, he is a new creature; the old things passed away; behold, new things have come" (2 Cor. 5:17).

Have you dwelt on thoughts of self-rejection? Have you believed the lie that you are worthless? Have you dwelt on thoughts of self-pity?

INFERIORITY

"Blessed be the God and Father of our Lord Jesus Christ, who has blessed us with every spiritual blessing in the heavenly places in Christ, just as He chose us in Him before the foundation of the world, that we would be holy and blameless before Him" (Eph. 1:3-4).

Have you dwelt on thoughts of inferiority? Have you failed to believe how valuable you are to God? Have you been more concerned about what people think of you rather than what Jesus Christ thinks of you? Have you been overly self-conscious?

MURDER

"Everyone who hates his brother is a murderer; and you know that no murderer has eternal life abiding in him" (1 John 3:15).

Have you ever murdered anyone? Do you fantasize about murdering someone? Have you ever wished someone was dead? Have you ever attempted suicide? Have you dwelt on thoughts of suicide?

ABORTION

> *"There are six things which the LORD hates, Yes, seven which are an abomination to Him: Haughty eyes, a lying tongue, And hands that shed innocent blood" (Prov. 6:16-17).*

Have you ever had an abortion? Have you ever encouraged or assisted someone in having an abortion?

PREJUDICE

> *"He [Jesus] also told this parable to some people who trusted in themselves that they were righteous, and viewed others with contempt: 'Two men went up into the temple to pray, one a Pharisee and the other a tax collector. The Pharisee stood and was praying this to himself, God, I thank You that I am not like other people: swindlers, unjust, adulterers, or even like this tax collector'" (Luke 18:9-11).*

Have you ever been prejudiced toward people of a different race? Have you looked down at others who are different than you? Have you been prejudiced against those who are overweight? Have you shown hatred or been violent towards homosexuals? Have you been prejudiced toward people who have more, or less money than you? Do you judge people who dress differently, have longer or shorter hair than you, or have tattoos?

HARMFUL MUSIC

"Let the word of Christ richly dwell within you, with all wisdom teaching and admonishing one another with psalms and hymns and spiritual songs, singing with thankfulness in your hearts to God" (Col. 3:16).

Have you willfully listened to music which had immoral lyrics? Have you idolized a musician who you knew was on drugs or had an immoral lifestyle?

SEXUAL IMMORALITY

"Flee immorality. Every other sin that a man commits is outside the body, but the immoral man sins against his own body" (1 Cor. 6:18).

Have you committed sexual sin? Have you entertained sexual fantasies? Have you looked at pornography? Have you seen a movie or video that had an immoral scene?

ADULTERY

"Marriage is to be held in honor among all, and the marriage bed is to be undefiled; for fornicators and adulterers God will judge" (Heb. 13:4).

Have you ever committed adultery? Have you ever committed fornication? Have you fantasized about having sex with someone other than your spouse?

INCEST

"If there is a man who lies with his daughter in-law, both of them shall surely be put to death; they have committed incest, their bloodguiltiness is upon them" (Lev. 20:12).

Have you committed incest? Have you dwelt on thoughts of committing incest? Have you ever sexually abused a child?

HOMOSEXUALITY

"For this reason God gave them over to degrading passions; for their women exchanged the natural function for that which is unnatural, and in the same way also the men abandoned the natural function of the woman and burned in their desire toward one another, men with men committing indecent acts and receiving in their own persons the due penalty of their error" (Rom. 1:26-27).

Have you allowed thoughts of homosexual or lesbian behavior to linger in your mind? Have you yielded to thoughts of same sex attraction? Have you ever engaged in homosexual or lesbian acts?

GUILT

"There is now no condemnation for those who are in Christ Jesus" (Rom. 8:1).

Have you condemned yourself for your past sins? Have you

failed to believe that God is willing to forgive you of every sin you have ever committed? Do you condemn yourself because you think that you have failed others? Have you submitted to thoughts of guilt because you think that you have failed as a parent?

FEAR

"There is no fear in love; but perfect love casts out fear, because fear involves punishment, and the one who fears is not perfected in love" (1 John 4:18).

Have you allowed your mind to dwell on thoughts of irrational fears? Do you have a fear of death or a fear of sickness? Are you afraid of Satan or demons? Are you afraid of the dark or heights?

WORRY

"Be anxious for nothing, but in everything by prayer and supplication with thanksgiving let your requests be made known to God" (Phil. 4:6).

Do you worry? Do you rationalize your worry by calling it merely concern? Have you worried about what other people think of you? Do you worry that you may get sick? Do you worry about your children or your parents? Have you worried about finances? Do you worry about losing your job or being laid off? Have you failed to believe that it is God who provides your physical and material needs?

REBELLION

"Rebellion is as the sin of divination, And insubordination is as iniquity and idolatry. Because you have rejected the word of the LORD, He has also rejected you from being king" (1 Sam. 15:23).

Have you been rebellious? Have you rebelled against your parents? Have you rebelled against school authority, police, or other civic authority? Do you have a rebellious attitude toward your pastor or other spiritual leaders in the church? Are you rebelling against what you know God wants you to do or stop doing?

HUSBANDS AND WIVES

"As the church is subject to Christ, so also the wives ought to be to their husbands in everything. Husbands, love your wives, just as Christ also loved the church and gave Himself up for her" (Eph. 5:24-25).

Husbands, have you failed to love your wife as Jesus Christ loves the church? Have you failed to make sacrifices for your wife? Wives, have you failed to be submissive to your husbands in everything that is not directly contrary to the Word of God? Do you treat your spouse as if he or she has no value or worth? Have you tried to control your spouse? Have you hidden financial information from your spouse?

DRUGS

"I urge you, brethren, by the mercies of God, to present your bodies a living and holy sacrifice, acceptable to God, which is your spiritual service of worship. And do not be conformed to this world, but be transformed by the renewing of your mind, that you may prove what the will of God is, that which is good and acceptable and perfect" (Rom. 12:1-2).

Have you ever used illegal drugs? Have you abused prescription drugs? Have you used mind altering drugs for recreational purposes even if they are legal?

WITCHCRAFT

"There shall not be found among you anyone who makes his son or his daughter pass through the fire, one who uses divination, one who practices witchcraft, or one who interprets omens, or a sorcerer, or one who casts a spell, or a medium, or a spiritist, or one who calls up the dead" (Deut. 18:10-11).

Have you ever been involved with witchcraft, Satanism, fortune telling, or astral projection? Have you ever been involved in visualization or palm reading? Have you ever tried to develop ESP or Ki? Have you ever participated in an animal or human sacrifice?

ASTROLOGY

"You are wearied with your many counsels; Let now the astrologers, Those who prophesy by the stars, Those who predict by the new moons, Stand up and save you from what will come upon you" (Isa. 47:13).

Have you ever been involved with astrology? Have you ever read your horoscope, even just for fun?

CHANNELING

"When they say to you, 'Consult the mediums and the spiritists who whisper and mutter,' should not a people consult their God? Should they consult the dead on behalf of the living?" (Isa. 8:19).

Have you ever consulted a psychic or a medium? Have you ever participated in a seance? Have you ever played with a ouija board? Have you ever asked for guidance from any spirit other than the Holy Spirit?

OCCULT OBJECTS

"Many of those who practiced magic brought their books together and began burning them in the sight of everyone; and they counted up the price of them and found it fifty thousand pieces of silver" (Acts 19:19).

Have you ever read or possessed occult books? Have you ever possessed occult objects or jewelry? Have you ever possessed a ouija board, tarot cards, or a crystal ball?

FALSE RELIGIONS

"I am afraid that, as the serpent deceived Eve by his craftiness, your minds will be led astray from the simplicity and purity of devotion to Christ. For if one comes and preaches another Jesus whom we have not preached, or you receive a different spirit which you have not received, or a different gospel which you have not accepted, you bear this beautifully" (2 Cor. 11:3-4).

Have you ever been involved with Buddhism, Hinduism, Jehovah's Witnesses, Mormonism, New Age, or any other false religion or philosophy?

VIOLENCE

"The LORD tests the righteous and the wicked, And the one who loves violence His soul hates" (Ps. 11:5).

Have you dwelt on thoughts of violence? Have you watched movies or videos for entertainment that had violent scenes? Have you ever been involved in karate or other martial arts where meditation was taught? Have you ever visualized punching, kicking, killing, or sexually attacking someone?

INTERNET AND MEDIA

"Whether, then, you eat or drink or whatever you do, do all to the glory of God" (1 Cor. 10:31).

Have you wasted time with television, videos, movies, internet, and social media? Is your time with God cut short because you prefer time on the internet? Do you view material or visit sites that do not glorify God?

PRACTICAL SUGGESTIONS

Allowing the Holy Spirit to take an inventory of your life can take an extraordinary amount of time. It is not unusual to be convicted by the Holy Spirit of dozens of sins in any particular sin category. Thus, it is improbable that a person could pray through the Sinventory in one evening. It could take weeks or even months to complete. Furthermore, it is not sufficient to merely read the Sinventory if you truly desire to experience personal revival. Instead, after each verse and comment is read, the believer should ask God to reveal any sin that exists in his or her life. Without prayer and the leadership of the Holy Spirit, the believer will become overly introspective, which can lead to self-condemnation.

Believers can become discouraged when their lives are compared to the absolute standard of the Word of God. However, the believer only deceives himself when he justifies unrepented sin. It is sin that often hinders the believer from experiencing love, joy, and peace. Although sin sometimes brings temporary pleasure, it always brings eventual sorrow. Believers must submit their life to the authority of the Word of God and be honest with themselves if they desire to have intimate fellowship with God and experience personal revival.

Finally, the believer should never condemn himself regardless of the type or amount of sin that has been committed. Jesus Christ has paid the penalty for the believer's sin. This is why the Apostle Paul stated, "There is now no condemnation for those who are in Christ Jesus" (Rom.

8:1). God no longer condemns the believer for his sin; therefore, neither should the believer condemn himself. The Holy Spirit convicts the believer of sin to allow him the opportunity to repent so the sin that is hindering the fullness and blessing of God can be removed. The wonderful truth revealed in the Bible is God has promised that He is willing to extend His grace to the believer no matter how great the sin or the number of sins in their life.

NOTES

1. William J. Petersen, *25 Surprising Marriages* (Grand Rapids, MI: Baker Books, 1997), p. 24.

2. The literal meaning of Abaddon in Hebrew is destruction. Apollyon in Greek means "destroyer." Merrill F. Unger, *Unger's Bible Dictionary* (Chicago, IL: Moody Press, 1983), pp. 2 and 72.

3. "The present tense of the verb in the imperative denotes a 'continuous or repeated' action so that the meaning is 'keep on being filled,' or 'be constantly filled.'" Merrill F. Unger, *The Baptism & Gifts of the Holy Spirit* (Chicago, IL: Moody Press, 1980), p. 29.

4. John Nicholas Lenker, *Luther's Catechetical Writing* (Minneapolis, MN: The Luther Press, 1907), p. 305.

5. Herbert Lockyer, *All the Promises of the Bible*, Grand Rapid, MI: Zondervan Publishing House, 1975), p. 9. (Everet R. Storms, a Canadian Schoolteacher, during his 27th reading of the Bible counted 8,810 promises).

6. W.E. Vine, Merrill F. Unger, and William White, Jr., *Vine's Complete Expository Dictionary* (Nashville, TN:

Thomas Nelson, 1996), p. 613 (Machaira means "a short sword or dagger").

7. The word myriad means 10,000. *New American Standard, Exhaustive Concordance of the Bible, Hebrew-Aramaic and Greek Dictionaries* (Nashville, TN: Holman, 1981), p. 1594.

8. Archimedes was a mathematician in the 3rd century B.C. In an ancient work entitled The Sand Reckoner, Archimedes sought to determine the number of grains of sands that the universe could contain and used the term myriad in his analysis. Translation of *The Sand Reckoner* reprinted in James R. Newman, *World of Mathematics*, Vol. 1 (Redmond, WA: Tempus Books 1988), pp. 411-419.

9. Heinrichs, Allison M., "How Many Stars in Universe? 70 Sextillion," *Orlando Sentinel*, July 25, 2003.

10. Billy Graham seems to imply that the supernatural being that struck the 185,000 men in the camp of the Assyrians was an angel. Billy Graham, *Angels – God's Secret Agents* (Nashville, TN: Thomas Nelson, 1994), p. 96. Keep in mind, it could be that "the angel of the Lord" is a reference to the pre-incarnate Jesus Christ and not a holy angel. W.E. Vine, Merrill F. Unger, and William White, Jr., *Vine's Complete Expository Dictionary* (Nashville, TN: Thomas Nelson, 1996), p. 5 ("The relation between the Lord and the 'angel of the Lord' is often so close that it is difficult to separate the two… This identification has led some interpreters to conclude that the 'angel of the Lord' was the pre-incarnate Christ").

11. C. Fred Dickason, *Angels - Elect & Evil* (Chicago, IL: Moody Press, 1995), p. 89.

12. J. Edwin Hartill, *Principles of Biblical Hermeneutics* (Grand Rapids, MI: Zondervan Publishing House, 1947), p. 105.

13. Billy Graham, *Angels – God's Secret Agents*, p. 59; C. Fred Dickason, *Angels - Elect & Evil*, p. 143.

14. *New American Standard, Exhaustive Concordance of the Bible, Hebrew-Aramaic and Greek Dictionaries*, p. 1688.

15. *See e.g.*, Matt 8:16, Matt. 8:28, Matt. 9:32, Matt. 12:22, Matt. 15:22, Mark 1:32, and Luke 8:36 in the King James and New American Standard versions of the Bible.

16. Merrill F. Unger, *What Demons Can Do to Saints* (Chicago, IL: Moody, 1977), p. 86.

17. C. Fred Dickason, *Demon Possession & the Christian* (Westchester, IL: Crossway Books, 1987).

18. Daniel L. Akin (ed.), *A Theology for the Church* (Nashville, TN: B&H Academic, 2007), p. 134.

19. *New American Standard, Exhaustive Concordance of the Bible, Hebrew-Aramaic and Greek Dictionaries*, p. 1616.

20. Neil T. Anderson, *The Bondage Breaker* (Eugene, OR: Harvest House Publishers, 1993), p. 205 ("The last step to freedom is to renounce the sins of your ancestors…"); Edward F. Murphy, *Spiritual Warfare Handbook* (Nashville, TN: Thomas Nelson Publishers, Inc.,

1992), p. 438 ("Thus, it is wise to confess the sins of one's family line").

21. *See e.g.,* Gal. 3:13, Rom. 4:15, Rom. 8:1-4, and I Thess. 5:9.

22. Neil T. Anderson, The Bondage Breaker, pp. 205-206 ("The fact that demonic strongholds can be passed on from one generation to the next is well-attested by those who counsel the afflicted").

23. Edward F. Murphy, *Spiritual Warfare Handbook*, p. 437 ("To my knowledge, direct and clearly defined biblical teaching or examples of demonic transference are not found in Scripture").

24. Nothing in this book should be interpreted or construed to suggest, imply, direct, or recommend that a person should not seek immediate and appropriate professional medical or psychological services in treating an emotional, physical, or mental challenge.

www.ingramcontent.com/pod-product-compliance
Lightning Source LLC
Chambersburg PA
CBHW060900120626
46553CB00001B/156